Communication Skills
for
Collaborative Learning

Second Edition

James A. Luotto
De Anza College

Edwina L. Stoll
De Anza College

Mia Hoglund-Kettmann
De Anza College

KENDALL/HUNT PUBLISHING COMPANY
4050 Westmark Drive   Dubuque, Iowa 52002

Copyright © 1995, 2001 by Kendall/Hunt Publishing Company

ISBN 0-7872-8801-2

Printed in the United States of America
10 9 8 7 6 5 4 3 2 1

CONTENTS

PREFACE

We believe that increasing awareness of and proficiency in communication skills will enhance student participation in classes using the **Collaborative Learning Method**. In support of that belief we have prepared a workbook with a dual purpose: to teach communication skills which specifically translate into collaborative activities, and to offer a variety of collaborative classroom activities that can be adapted for use across the academic disciplines. In our Letter to Instructors found in Part I we have included descriptions of several collaborative activity structures, a list of things to consider when forming class groups, and some advice for starting to use collaborative learning in any class.

To introduce the Second Edition of this workbook we have collaborated with a third author, Mia Hoglund-Kettmann, who has used these materials for several years and recently joined the De Anza faculty as a full-time instructor. Mia brings a rich multicultural perspective that you will easily find infused throughout the pages and specifically in some of the new collaborative assignments that directly address multicultural issues. We continue to collaborate with many instructors whose materials and assignments we are pleased to again include in this new edition. As with our previous editions, we are proud to showcase examples from our students. In this edition, each major assignment is followed by at least one student example.

This workbook can be used in any course -- in any discipline -- in which the values and skills of the **Collaborative Learning Method** are desired:

- o **emphasis on student responsibility for and commitment to his or her own learning.**

- o **emphasis on community and mutual responsibility in the learning process.**

- o **reading and workshop training in the skills needed for successful use of the collaborative method:**

    - **Reflective Listening and Active Listening**

    - **Clear Sending and Congruent Sending**

    - **Developing High Synergy**

    - **Supporting Teammates**

    - **Problem Solving and Consensus Decision Making**

PART I *Introduction*

A LETTER TO STUDENTS

Dear Students using our workbook:

What is the Collaborative Learning Model?

This workbook uses an approach to learning which is not really new, because it uses the basic ways people, including you, have always learned. But it may be new to you in the academic environment, so we would like to introduce you to some assumptions that are basic to the collaborative method:

1. **In order to learn, you must take necessary and appropriate <u>risks</u>.**

If you agree with this statement, you have probably already thought of examples. If not, here's one we're all familiar with: <u>learning to ride a bicycle</u>. If you think about it, a child (which is what most of us were when we learned this skill) must *really* want to learn to ride a bike to get on such an unstable platform, traveling at a speed faster than she or he can run, on <u>cement</u>, without even knowing how to steer!

And you can't learn to ride a bike without taking the risk of falling and hurting yourself.

Can you learn by watching someone else -- <u>a teacher</u>, in the form of a parent, or older sister, or brother -- ride a bike, to show you how it should be done? That would help; it would certainly encourage you. But, in the final analysis, <u>you</u> must get on the bike.

That is how it will be in this course.

What if I don't want to take the necessary risks?

That doesn't make you a bad person. It just means you will never learn whatever it was that would require the risks that you are refusing to take. That's why many people never learn to hang-glide, or speak a foreign language, or change jobs, or any number of things: They decided that they weren't willing to take the necessary risks. And that's fine! As long as the choice is understood.

What kinds of risks are we talking about in this speech communication course?

Here are a few:

In Interpersonal Communication ("one-on-one")
Someone might not like you; or ignore you; or find you strange, or weak, or misguided.

In Group Communication ("one-to-a few")
Others might disagree with you; you might be misunderstood; you might be wrong.

In Public Speaking (Communication) ("one-to-the whole group")
You might make a fool of yourself.

These are the kinds of fears that keep people from taking the necessary risks required to learn the skills included in this workbook. **We invite you to take them.**

2.   You may study alone, but you learn in a community.

A class becomes a community when you are with other people who are striving for the same goals that you are, in a situation that involves challenge and risk-taking. Athletes, musicians, and actors know how strong and real such communities can be, even if they are only temporary.

Though you will generally study and prepare by yourself, the individual class sessions are "workshops," in which you will be practicing with and learning from each other. It is only with others that you can learn and test and practice the skills of the course. And there is no better way to learn than to try to help and teach others. Ask any teacher, and they will tell you this.

Another term for this idea of learning with each other is "high synergy," a concept that we will be studying in the group communication section of the course.

3.   Learning requires assertiveness.

All communication, whether "interpersonal," in a "group," or alone in a formal "speech," can be seen as existing along a continuum.

PASSIVE	ASSERTIVE	AGGRESSIVE

This concept will be given much attention during the course, but to state it simply, in terms of legitimate _needs_: If I am _passive_, I am afraid to take the risk necessary to meet my own needs. If I am _aggressive,_ then I meet my needs, but at your expense. If I am _assertive,_ then I am willing to take the necessary risk to meet my own needs while trying to be sensitive to yours.

The goal for good communication -- and, therefore, for this course -- is:

assertive communication,

whether in interpersonal, group, or public communication situations.

Ours is a country rich in ethnic diversity, which is a great resource, if we are open, sensitive, and assertive. It is also a challenge. One of the real values of a collaborative class is that it provides an opportunity to work very closely with a variety of people, each with his or her own interpersonal style. But you must be assertive enough to take this opportunity that the class presents. Do your best to resist the natural, but essentially passive, inclination to work only with those you feel comfortable or "safe" with. _Learn from others and discover yourself._

Sincerely,

Jim Luotto, Edwina Stoll, and Mia Hoglund-Kettmann
De Anza College
Cupertino, California

ASSIGNMENT: Student Information Sheet

NAME_____ SS# _____ - ___ - _____

ADDRESS_____CITY_____ZIP_____

PHONE DAY:_____   EMAIL_____
PHONE EVENING:_____

What is your history at this school? Are you just entering? Are you working toward a degree?

What other formal Speech Communication classes have you taken? These may be from your high school or previous college or work experience. Please name the course and describe the types of projects you did.

When you have finished school what sort of a career will you pursue?

How do you rate yourself as a communicator? Give an example of a situation in which you know you communicate well (you feel success), and also an example of a situation in which you wish to improve your communication skills.

Have you seen yourself on videotape?   YES   NO   If yes, describe.

Tell me a bit about yourself. (hobbies, interests, family)

A LETTER TO INSTRUCTORS

Dear Colleagues:

We are all familiar with the adage; "You never really learn something until you try to teach it." And we believe as teachers that we know the statement to be true. Ironically, however, in the traditional classroom structure, we, as the "teachers," necessarily reserve this special learning status for ourselves, and place the students in the relatively passive status of the "learners." Thus, we often feel at cross-purposes with our students: "Why don't they want to learn, when there is so much of value that I want to teach them?" We sense a distance between ourselves and the students, a "void." When we try to fill this void with our own energy, we have the frustrating, disturbing feeling that we're doing most of the work in the classroom. We are!

The Collaborative Learning method attempts to correct this situation by shifting, **as much as possible,** the responsibility for the teaching -- and, therefore, the learning -- process from the teacher to the student.

What is the Collaborative Learning model?

Here are some of the basic values:

1. You may study alone, but you learn in a community.

2. In order to learn, you must take necessary and appropriate <u>risks</u>.

3. The basic metaphor of **getting** an education is inaccurate, misleading, since it implies that an education is somehow *external* to the learner, a goal one accomplishes after having successfully completed the required steps. It would be more accurate to speak of the student's giving an education. The essential dynamic of the learning process is **inside-out**, not **outside-in.** The curriculum and the classroom must accommodate this basic truth.

4. In the Collaborative Learning model, the **student group,** whether it is the entire class or smaller workshop groups of various sizes, is the basic focus of the classroom. The role of the teacher as "star performer" is diminished, though most certainly not eliminated. To put it in simplest terms, the students are as likely to be looking at each other, as they are to be looking at the teacher.

Does the Collaborative Learning model diminish the importance of the teacher?

On the contrary, because this model places the students in unfamiliar and challenging situations, the teacher, as mentor/model/evaluator/authority, becomes a more important presence than in the conventional setting. And the different learning modes within the classroom -- small- and large-group discussions, task-related workshop groups, formal and informal lectures,* etc. -- will present the teacher with a constant and varied challenge.

> *Ideally, lecturing will often be **interactive,** a response to issues and concerns generated by the students, not imposed on them. There will be other times, of course, when conventional lecturing is simply the most practical means of conveying information or explaining issues.

How does the Collaborative Learning method address these four values?

1.   You may study alone, but you learn in a community.

We believe that learning is not a private experience; study is often private, but learning is not. We learn from each other, from peers who affirm in various ways the value of the learning enterprise, as well as of our individual effort and ideas. As we look back on our own college experience, we are aware that we learned at least as much from discussion and work with classmates as we did from teachers and books. Because we lived on campus, there were more opportunities for such experiences.

But there are many pressures in contemporary society that undermine the students' chances for forming ongoing relationships with peers, for enjoying the intellectual "give-and-take" which should be central to the college experience. The fact is, most of our students really don't know each other at all, even in a superficial way.

The Collaborative Learning model restructures and refocuses the academic program to bring to students [and faculty!] these values of the "learning community."

We believe that the "learning community" is the best environment in which learning takes place, particularly at the community college level. Any number of studies led to the conclusion that students actually learn more from their peers than from any other source. Kenneth Bruffee, director of the Honors Program at Brooklyn College, in a summary of William Perry's book Forms of Intellectual and Ethical Development in the College Years, makes this point succinctly: "The central educational issues today hinge on social relations, not on cognitive ones: relations among persons, not relations between persons and things. Learning as we must understand it today. . .does not involve people's assimilation of knowledge, it involves people's assimilation into communities of knowledgeable peers."

But many of our students find themselves in a most abstract community: a kaleidoscopic aggregation of faces that fades and reforms course after course, quarter after quarter, as they get their education. It can often be a lonely experience. Ask the students, and they will agree. Perhaps loneliness is simply in the nature of the "commuter college" situation, which is what the majority of our students experience, despite the best intentions of the faculty to make it otherwise. We prefer not to accept this conclusion, believing instead that imaginative approaches can foster a sense of student and faculty community.

2.   **In order to learn, you must take necessary and appropriate risks.**

Collaborative learning, depending as it does on communication skills, makes necessary assumptions about students' ability to work cooperatively, to "collaborate" in the learning process. Students must be required to consistently practice basic communication skills. Equally important, faculty must consistently model these skills themselves. But communication skills don't just come "naturally"; they have to be learned. In fact, to many of the students, these skills often seem "unnatural" at first. To quote Kenneth Bruffee once again, "Collaborative learning has to begin in most cases with an attempt to **re-acculturate** students. Given most students' almost exclusively traditional experience, they have to learn, sometimes against considerable resistance, to grant authority to a peer instead of to the teacher. Skillfully organized collaborative learning can itself re-acculturate students in this way."

Because domination by the aggressive few and silence by the passive many are destructive to the collaborative process, in order for collaborative learning to be successful, students must learn basic speaking and, especially, listening skills. Communication skills that promote assertive participation must be taught from the start and continually encouraged.

Teaching habits that inhibit assertive risk-taking in the classroom must be changed. For example, the instructor should avoid asking questions for which there is a "right" answer, thereby confusing the open-ended examination of an idea with quizzing under the guise of "discussion." Students' willingness to risk diminishes inversely with their need to be "correct." **Avoid ambiguity:** If you want to test students' knowledge, give a quiz. If you want to be sure that students have some important information, tell them what they need to know, rather than "fishing" to see which students already possess these facts.

3.	**The essential dynamic of the learning process is inside-out, not outside-in. Get the students to "buy into" the activities of the day as well as "buy into" the broader goals of the course.**

On a day-to-day basis, encourage student responsibility in the discussion of assignments by giving students precisely-defined small group tasks to be accomplished prior to the teacher-directed discussions with the entire class. These activities not only encourage the less assertive, by virtually requiring participation at a less-threatening "small group" level, but they also get a degree of student commitment to the day's activities.

In regards to the long-term goals of the class, structure activities in such a way that students see each other as significant participants in the learning process. In the De Anza College Collaborative Learning Speech 10 Class [Fundamentals of Oral Communication], for example, students are formed into on-going "Speech Support Groups" which provide constructive criticism and encouragement in the challenging, potentially threatening, process of planning and presenting speeches.

4.	**Since the students assume much of the responsibility for each other's learning, activities must be precisely structured. Students cannot be expected to share the burden for the conduct and success of the various activities, unless their tasks are carefully defined. Far from being "free form," the Collaborative Learning class hour must be as precise as possible, in both design and execution.**

In collaborative learning the students are encouraged to be active agents in the classroom experience, rather than simply being recipients, however well motivated. Students in such a program are encouraged to teach each other, to cooperate in the learning process, to share insights, knowledge, and enthusiasms. In a college where students reside on campus, this can be achieved informally and is central to the college experience. In a "commuter college," such experiences are, at best, difficult for the students to accomplish. Thus, the experiences must be designed into the curriculum, if they are to happen on any meaningful scale.

A Final Note

To assist you in planning and structuring your class activities we have included in this introductory section three readings that have guided us over the years. They are "Formats for Group Work" compiled by Barbara Millis, "Some Considerations for forming Class Groups" which we composed together, and "Getting Started" by Susan Prescott.

For ten years we have been working collaboratively to design and teach our classes, and in the preparation and sharing of the materials which comprise this workbook. As you begin to teach using this workbook, we invite you to join our collaborative group -- as teachers. We hope that you will call us at De Anza College with your questions, suggestions, ideas, or just to visit with us. We welcome you to the team!

Sincerely,

Jim Luotto, Edwina Stoll, and Mia Hoglund-Kettmann
De Anza College
Cupertino, California

Formats for Group Work

This list of group work formats was compiled by Barbara Millis, based on her workshops for the Teaching and Learning Center at the University of Nebraska, Lincoln (Nov. 5, 1990) and her presentation at the national conference of the POD Network in Higher Education (October 1993). This list reprinted with permission from the Teaching at UNL newsletter (Vol. 15, No. 4, February 1994), produced by the Teaching and Learning Center at the University of Nebraska, Lincoln.

Think-Pair-Share

The instructor poses a question, preferably one demanding analysis, evaluation, or synthesis, and gives students at least a minute to think through an appropriate response. This time can also be spent writing.

Students then turn to a partner and share their responses. Then, student responses can be shared within a four-person learning team, within a larger group, or with the entire class in a follow-up discussion, and all students can learn by reflection and verbalization.

Three-Step Interview

Common as an icebreaker or team-building exercise, this structure can be used also to share information, such as hypotheses or reactions to a film or article.

Students interview each other in pairs, alternating roles. They then share in a four-member learning team what they learned from the paired interview.

Numbered Heads Together

Members of learning teams, usually composed of four individuals, count off: 1, 2, 3, or 4. The instructor poses a question, usually factual in nature, but requiring some higher-order thinking skills.

Students discuss the question, making certain that every group member knows the answer. The instructor calls a specific number and the designated team members respond as group spokespersons.

Again, students benefit from the verbalization, and the peer coaching helps both the high and the low achievers. Class time is usually better spent because less time is wasted on inappropriate responses and because all students become actively involved with the material. Since no one knows which number will be called, all team members have a vested interest in understanding the appropriate response.

Roundtable

The students write in turn on a single pad of paper, stating their ideas aloud as they write. As the tablet circulates, more and more information is added until various aspects of a topic are explored.

Talking Chips

To structure discussion and encourage full participation, each team member contributes to the discussion after placing a talking chip (pen, checker, index card, etc.) in the center of the group. After all students have contributed in random order, they retrieve their chips to begin another round.

Co-op Cards

Useful for memorization and review, students coach each other using flashcards.

Simple Jigsaw

The instructor divides an assignment or topic into four parts, with each student from each team volunteering to become an "expert" on one of the parts. "Experts" on a given topic then work together to master their fourth of the material and to discover the best way to help others learn it. All "experts" then reassemble in their home learning teams, where they teach the other group members.

From *Teaching at UNL*, Vol. 15, No. 4, February 1994 by Barbara Millis. Reprinted by permission of Dr. Barbara Millis.

Structured Controversy

Team members assume different positions on controversial issues, then discuss, research, and share their findings with the group. This technique lets students explore topics in depth and promotes higher-order thinking skills.

Group Investigation

In six stages, groups investigate topics of mutual interest, planning what they will study, how they will divide the research responsibilities, and how they will synthesize and summarize their findings for the class.

Send-a-Problem

Each team member makes up a review question and writes it on a card (label Q), then asks other members of the group to answer it. If there is total consensus on the answer, it is written on the back of the card (label A).

After all questions and answers are discussed and recorded, the stack of cards is passed to another group. Members of the next group discuss one question and come to consensus on the answer. Then they turn the card over to see if it agrees with the original group's answer. If not, they record their answer on the card as an alternative. The procedure is repeated. The stacks of cards can be sent to a third and fourth group, etc.

Finally, they are returned to the senders, who can clarify any questions indicated on the A-side of the card.

Value Lines

You can use value lines to get students to evaluate their positions. Each student lines up according to how strongly he or she agrees or disagrees with some statement/proposition, or how strongly he or she values something. Once students are lined up, they have a visual reading of the continuum of feelings in the group.

An additional sharing of views will result if students are paired so that an end person (#1) pairs with a middle person (#11 in a group of 20), with this pairing continuing (#2 and #12, etc.) until all are paired (see example below).

Example: Group Formation With a Value Line
Step 1. Form a rank-ordered line and number participants (males, females) as follows:

Strong Agreement																		Strong Disagreement	
1	2	3	4	5	6	7	8	9	10	11	12	13	14	15	16	17	18	19	20
m	f	m	f	m	f	m	f	m	f	m	f	m	f	m	f	m	f	m	f

Step 2. Form heterogeneous groups of four by assigning the above numbered participants as follows:

Group #1				Group #2				Group #3				Group #4				Group #5			
1	10	11	20	2	9	12	19	3	8	13	18	4	7	14	17	5	6	15	16
m	f	m	f	f	m	f	m	m	f	m	f	f	m	f	m	m	f	m	f

Active Listening

This builds on the value line format and then asks one student to explain his or her position for one minute, while the partner listens and then tries to paraphrase. Then partners switch roles.

Some Considerations for Forming Class Groups

The responsibility for forming class groups rests with the instructor. The instructor should form groups based on the goals of the group work and the length of time the group will need to work together. For example, if the goal of the group work is to brainstorm a list of some sort and the length of time the group will work together will be during only 20 or 30 minutes of one class period, then the instructor may simply ask the students to form themselves in to groups of 4 or 5 members. On, the other hand, if the goal is a problem solving activity during which time the groups will meet for three weeks both inside and outside of class time, the instructor may wish to form the class groups after considering some or all of the following possibilities.

Group Size

The experts tell us that the best group size for most tasks is between 3 and 6 members. Sometimes there are reasons to form a larger group or to let the students work in dyads. Generally speaking, the larger the group the longer the task will take to complete. On the other hand, smaller groups generate fewer ideas and sometimes become stymied if just one group member happens to be absent.

Type of Activity or Task

To form groups in class it is important to consider the level of difficulty in the assignment the group will need to perform. Matching the difficulty level with the length of time the group will have to complete the assignment will help in setting up class groups.

Student Attributes

Sometimes there is a reason to form the group based on the ability levels of the students. For example, a writing instructor may mix the ability levels of the group members so that those with stronger writing skills will be able to assist those with weaker skills. Other attributes to consider in group formation are gender, ethnicity, age, etc. An instructor we know forms groups for an out-of-class assignment by placing those together who live in the same area of the city, so they might be able to meet more easily.

Student Preferences

Students may be asked to rank order a list of topics or to list their interests as a way of forming groups. Some instructors ask students to list one or two names of their classmates who they would like to work with, and one or two whom they would prefer not to work with. Using this type of sociogram to consider group membership can help make the students more vested in the group because they had a say in the group formation.

Getting Started in Group Work

Susan Prescott, Ed.D., Professor of Education at the California State University Dominguez Hills, wrote the following article which we have included here because it offers wonderful advice for instructors who want to organize groups/teams in their classrooms and it includes two helpful examples of ways for the groups to keep records once they are organized. This article, along with several others that Susan has written, appeared in the Newsletter for the Network of Cooperative Learning and College Teaching. (Reprinted with permission.)

The successful application of Cooperative Learning (CL) in the classroom requires careful attention to details of implementation that can be easily overlooked. I will describe how a team folder can work to help both the instructor and student feel more organized and productive. Folders also seem to provide a greater feeling of team identity for students.

Once teams are formed, I give each group a file folder with their names on the outside. The three classes I teach meet once a week for three hours and are color-coded. Monday's folders are red; Wednesday's, blue; and Thursday's yellow. In this way I can immediately identify which stack of folders to take to class or which folders I need in order to insert the papers I want to return to students. The folders function as an important channel of communication. All homework, notes, projects, and tests can be turned in and returned using the folders. I tape each team's Polaroid photo on the folder cover; it's fun, the students love it, and the team monitor can locate his team's folders quickly. An alternative might be to have the students bring in personal photos or put a team insignia on the cover.

Pages 15 and 17 are two important data sheets. The first is a chart describing the team roles and responsibilities; the second is a record-keeping chart on which information about students' attendance, homework, tests, and points for team practice activities is recorded.

Some faculty use a less-structured format called Collaborative Learning that does not incorporate any roles. However, most of my colleagues feel that roles help students stay on task, feel more organized, and increase the involvement of all members. Role titles can be traditional or creative. The only requirement is that the responsibilities for each role are made clear to the students.

Some faculty let students choose who will take each role. I prefer to assign all the roles the first time; students find out their roles when I hand out the team folders with names already filled in. A colleague of mine assigns the leader role based on prior highest GPA and lets the team self-select the remaining roles. He assigns each student a preplanned number on the day teams are formed and then tells them that all the number ones are the team leaders. None of these strategies seem to meet with resistance; once students know the rationale and see the benefits they are usually grateful and enthusiastic. The frequency of class meetings during the week may determine if or how often roles are rotated throughout the semester. My classes meet once a week for three hours, so I give each team the option of keeping or changing their team roles.

Some faculty members are concerned about the issue of record keeping and wonder how much is necessary and if it will be time-consuming. There seems to be a minimal amount of record keeping required, and students can manage it themselves. You only need to provide them with the folder and an explanation of how the chart is to be used. The team's recorder is responsible for entering all the data for test grades and bonus points for each practice activity that meets the criteria. Because my students are asked to sit with their teams upon entering the classroom, information gathering happens quickly and quietly at the start of class.

The record sheet is only an example and can be changed in any way to suit the maturity level of the students and the policies of the instructor. The days that the class meets are circled and attendance is taken each day. A new sheet will need to be stapled in the start of the sixth week of CL. The recorder can also record a plus or minus in the homework category; this section of the chart can be eliminated if not appropriate, but some students report that it makes them feel more accountable. If during any week the teams complete a practice activity that is worth a small amount of bonus points (much easier to award points than grades), then the recorder looks at the paper returned by the instructor in the team folder to see the number of points earned. These are then recorded in the box at the bottom of the chart. If a student is absent during any week in which a team activity was completed for points, the student's total semester score does not include those particular points when the instructor adds bonus points to each student's individual point total at the end of the semester.

Not all team tasks need to be turned in for bonus points. However the amount of points needs to be small (three to five) so that if the team tasks are worked on in class during the semester, the resulting thirty or fifty points won't significantly alter any student's overall point total that is used to compute the grade for the course. The principle of individual accountability is important and should not be violated by giving group grades.

The team folder is not a prerequisite to successfully implementing CL in the college classroom. However, it can be viewed as an optional strategy that can serve as a valuable motivational hook for students as well as a helpful management tool for instructors.

TEAM ROLES AND RESPONSIBILITIES

ROLES	NAMES		
	Round #1	Round #2	Round #3
LEADER			
1. MAKES SURE EVERYONE UNDERSTANDS THE NEW LEARNING AND ASSIGNMENT PROCEDURE			
2. ENSURES THAT ALL MEMBERS PARTICIPATE AND WORK PRODUCTIVELY			
3. FACILITATES RESOLUTION OF ANY CONFLICTS AMONG TEAM MEMBERS			
4. APPOINTS OR SERVES AS SUBSTITUTE FOR ANY ABSENT TEAM MEMBER (ON TEAMS OF FOUR)			
RECORDER			
1. RECORDS TEAM RESPONSES FOR PRESENTATION TO CLASS			
2. ENSURES THAT PRACTICE ACTIVITY IS COMPLETE IF ASSIGNMENT IS TO BE GIVEN TO INSTRUCTOR			
3. RECORDS ALL ABSENCES AND TEAM POINTS			
MONITOR			
1. PICKS UP AND RETURNS TEAM FOLDER			
2. ENSURES THAT ALL PAPERS IN FOLDER ARE DISTRIBUTED TO TEAMMATES			
3. MAKES A COPY OF CLASS NOTES FOR ABSENT MEMBER(S) AND CALLS BEFORE NEXT CLASS			
4. WRITES ABSENT MEMBERS' NAMES ON ALL HANDOUTS AND KEEPS IN TEAM FOLDER			
SPOKESPERSON			
1. MAKES SURE EVERYONE UNDERSTANDS ANSWERS/IDEAS TO BE SHARED			
2. REPORTS TEAM'S IDEAS TO CLASS (USES RECORDER'S NOTES WHEN NEEDED)			
SUBSTITUTE			
1. ASSUMES RESPONSIBILITIES FOR ANY ABSENT TEAM MEMBER			

TEAM RECORD

NAMES	Week #1 MTWTF	Week #2 MTWTF	Week #3 MTWTF	Week #4 MTWTF	Week #5 MTWTF
	ATTENDANCE				
1)					
2)					
3)					
4)					
5)					
	HOMEWORK				
1)					
2)					
3)					
4)					
5)					
	INDIVIDUAL ASSIGNMENTS - PROJECTS				
1)					
2)					
3)					
4)					
5)					
	TEAM PRACTICE ACTIVITIES				

BIBLIOGRAPHY

We have included this list of Bibliographic Readings, which we have found useful in our study of Collaborative Learning.

Bosworth, K. and Hamilton, S. J. (Eds.) Fall 1994. <u>Collaborative Learning: Underlying Processes and Effective Techniques</u>. New Directions for Teaching and Learning. 59. San Francisco: Jossey-Bass.

Bruffee, K. A. 1984. "Collaborative Learning and the `Conversation of Mankind.'" <u>College English</u>. 46: No. 7: 635-652.

Bruffee, K. A. 1993. <u>Collaborative Learning: Higher Education, Interdependence, and the Authority of Knowledge</u>. Baltimore, MD: The Johns Hopkins University Press.

Bruffee, K. A. 1973. "Collaborative Learning; Some Practical Models." <u>College English</u>. 34: 634-643.

Bruffee, K. A. 1987 May/June. "The Art of Collaborative Learning." <u>Change</u>.

Finkel, D. L. and Monk, G. S. 1983. "Teachers and Learning Groups: Dissolving the Atlas Complex." In Bouton, C. and Garth, R. Y. (Eds.) <u>Learning in Groups</u>. New Directions for Teaching and Learning. 14. San Francisco: Jossey-Bass.

Gabelnick, F. et al. 1990. "Learning Community Models" <u>Learning Communities: Creating Connections Among Students, Faculty, and Disciplines</u>. New Directions for Teaching and Learning Series Number 41 San Francisco: Jossey-Bass.

Goodsell, A., et al. (Eds.) 1992. <u>Collaborative Learning: A Sourcebook for Higher Education, Vol. I</u>. University Park, PA: National Center on Postsecondary Teaching, Learning, and Assessment.

Johnson, D. W., Johnson, R. T., and Smith, K. A. 1991. <u>Active Learning: Cooperation in the College Classroom</u>. Edina, MN: Interaction Book.

Kadel, S. and Keehner, J. A. (Eds.) 1994. <u>Collaborative Learning: A Sourcebook for Higher Education, Vol. II</u>. University Park, PA: National Center on Postsecondary Teaching, Learning, and Assessment.

Knox-Quinn, C. Oct. 1990. "Collaboration in the Writing Classroom: An Interview with Ken Kesey." <u>College Composition and Communication</u>. 41: No. 3: 309-317.

MacGregor, J. 1990-1991. "Collaborative Learning: Reframing the Classroom." <u>Teaching Excellence</u>. The Professional and Organizational Development Network in Higher Education. 2: No. 3.

MacGregor, J. 1990. "Collaborative Learning: Shared Inquiry as a Process of Reform" <u>The Changing Face of College Teaching</u>. New Directions for Teaching and Learning Series Number 47 San Francisco: Jossey-Bass.

Millis, B. (Ed.) May 1994. "Formats for Group Work." <u>The Teaching Professor</u>. Magna Publications. Madison, WI.

Prescott, S. Winter 1992. "Getting Started with Cooperative Learning." in the Newsletter of Cooperative Learning and College Teaching. 2: No. 2.

Rau, W. and Heyl, B. April 1990. "Humanizing the College Classroom: Collaborative Learning and Social Organization Among Students." <u>Teaching Sociology</u>. 18: 141-155.

Trimbur, J. Oct. 1989. "Consensus and Difference in Collaborative Learning." <u>College English</u>.

Whipple, W. R. 1987 "Collaborative Learning, Recognizing It When We See It" American Association of Higher Education Bulletin.

PART II *Interpersonal Communication*

INTRODUCTION

<u>Assertiveness</u>

Good communication requires assertiveness. All significant communication whether "interpersonal," in a "group," or alone in a formal "speech," requires that we take appropriate risks. That's why it is often so hard to do, especially to do well. Because this course focuses on communication skills, you will be asked many times to take the appropriate risks needed to become a more assertive, more successful communicator. We say asked because a person cannot be made to take risks. In communication, growth must come from within; it cannot be imposed from without. You must choose to take advantage of the many opportunities this course will give you to become more assertive. Admittedly, assertiveness is a North American cultural perspective. It is also a reality for all of us living in the United States.

This concept will be given much attention during the course, but to state it simply, in terms of legitimate needs:

If I am **passive**,   then I am afraid to take the risk necessary to meet my own needs.

If I am **aggressive**,   then I meet my needs, but at your expense.

If I am **assertive**,   then I am willing to take the necessary risk to meet my own needs while trying to be sensitive to yours.

Thus, interpersonal communication can be seen as existing along a continuum:

<u>**PASSIVE   ASSERTIVE   AGGRESSIVE**</u>

The goal for good interpersonal communication -- and, therefore, for this course -- is **assertive** communication, whether in interpersonal, group, or public communication situations.

<u>How does this class encourage assertiveness?</u>

1. By **speaking** skillfully:
    a. Clear Sending
    b. Congruent Sending

2. By **listening** skillfully:
    a. Reflective Listening
    b. Active Listening

3. By promoting **high synergy**

It is important to realize that all communication is, ultimately, on the level of feelings. For this reason, with everything you do for this class, be aware of your feelings as you anticipate the activity, as you actually do it, and as you reflect on the activity. Don't try to "label" the feeling as good or bad. The emotion is going to be there no matter what you call it. More helpful in terms of personal growth is whether or not the feelings associated with a particular situation are useful or not. If they are, then the behavior associated with those feelings should be encouraged. If, instead, the feelings get in the way of assertive risk-taking, then work on changing these unproductive communication habits. Such change is not easy, of course: first you must become aware of the need to change. Then you need to learn more useful communication behavior. Finally, you must be assertive enough to risk actually changing a familiar, but not helpful, behavior. **Such assertive change is the goal of this course.**

Interpersonal Communication

Let's take a brief look at how the need to take appropriate risks to be more assertive applies to interpersonal communication.

Interpersonal communication is "one-on-one" as with a wife or husband, with a brother or sister, or a parent, or a friend, a neighbor, a classmate, or someone at work.

What are the risks inherent in **interpersonal communication** that make it hard to be assertive?

If you knew my true feelings:

> you might laugh at me.
> > you might dislike me.
> > > you might think I'm weak.
> > > > you might try to talk me out of my feelings.
> > > > > you might use what you know against me.
> > > > > > you might reject me.
> > > > > > > you might ignore me.

Rather than take these risks, I may be **passive**, and keep my feelings hidden from you. Or I may be **aggressive**, letting you see only anger, or cynicism, or sarcasm, or nonstop joking, or blaming. But at either end of the continuum -- whether passive or aggressive -- it's really fear that is determining my behavior, fear that you might know me.

Contract of Confidentiality

Right from the start, we feel it's essential for everyone in the class to make an agreement with each other, a promise, an open **"contract"** of confidentiality. Since the risk of *self-disclosure* is the essence of interpersonal communication, then we must be confident that whatever is said in this class will stay here, and not be repeated anywhere else. In other words, whatever we hear in this course is *privileged* material, a "gift" from the speaker to the class. This trust also applies when we are working in smaller groups: if you are working in *dyads*, then whatever is said belongs to the two of you only. If you are working in a "Skills" group, then whatever you hear belongs to your group only. Self-disclosure means risk-taking; it also means openness and trust.

Can we all agree on this? This is a **contract** we all make with each other now.

24

GETTING ACQUAINTED ACTIVITIES

Here are some of the things we do to get "off and running." The goal of these initial activities is to quickly begin establishing the essential characteristics of the Collaborative Learning class: a sense of community (learning everyone's name is certainly a first step), assertiveness, and a willingness to take appropriate risks.

The Name Game

1. Students and teacher sit in one big circle, so that we can all see one another. Fill in the circle; no empty seats.

2. Here are the rules: Moving clockwise, each person says his or her first name, the first names of everyone who came before, and then his/her first name again. The instructor can decide who begins. Since the person who starts has no one who "came before," s/he just says, "My name is Joe"; the person to Joe's left says, "Mary: Joe, Mary;" the person to Mary's left then says, "Naveen: Joe, Mary, Naveen;" the person to Naveen's left, "Kevin: Joe, Mary, Naveen, Kevin;" "Yvonne: Joe, Mary, Naveen, Kevin, Yvonne;" and so on...until the last person is attempting to recall the names of everyone in class!

   a. **No writing the names down!** This has to be done from memory. Be assertive enough to take the appropriate risks to do the task.

   b. Obviously, there is a risk here that you will forget someone's name. That is why some feel a little anxiety about the game. If you simply can't recall a person's name, just ask the person and he or she will tell you. It's as simple as that. What is the worst that can happen? Your mind will go "blank." Were that to happen (it probably won't), just say so, and the remaining people in the circle will tell you their names. In any case, this is not a "contest." It's just a useful way to learn a lot of names in a hurry.

3. When the last person has repeated the names around the circle, there are some other things that can be done:

   a. See if someone from the beginning of the line (Joe, Mary, Naveen, Kevin, or Yvonne) thinks he or she can do most of the names and is willing to try. No one is going to be "called on," since that would prevent you from making the choice to take the risk of being assertive. If two people volunteer, one can act as a "consultant," in case the other person can't recall a name.

   b. Move to different places in the circle and see if someone is willing to volunteer to try recalling all the names.

   Note: In our classes we do some version of the Name Game each day for the first week or two in order to reinforce learning each other's names.

Milling Around

This activity encourages a little more assertiveness and willingness to "risk," which nudges people a little further from passive "safe" patterns.

Everyone stands up and starts "milling," -- just walking slowly and more or less aimlessly, around the middle of the room. (Be sure that the space inside the circle of chairs is completely cleared first!)

Round One

There are just **two rules** that must be followed:

1. Absolutely no talking.

2. Be sure you don't touch anyone. If you see that you are about to brush by someone, be sure to avoid this.

   (Keep this up until you're told to stop -- about 2 to 4 minutes)

Round Two

1. Do the same as before, only now the second rule is removed. If you should happen to brush by someone, that's ok.

2. No talking.

   (Keep this up until you're told to stop -- about 2 to 4 minutes)

Round Three

1. This time, go to <u>each person</u>, and each person says the other person's name. If you can't remember the other person's name, just say so and the other person will tell you what his or her name is.

2. While you're saying the person's name, make some physical contact (whatever the instructor suggests: grab both hands of the person, or place your hand on the person's shoulder, etc.; try to avoid just "shaking hands.") **Be sure you get to everyone! Look around to be sure.**

   (When the entire group is done, return to your seats in the circle.)

<u>Introductions</u>

This opening activity is a good way to get to know everyone better and it also gives everyone some early experience in speaking before an audience. The instructor will divide the class into *dyads*, or pairs. The job of each dyad is to introduce itself to the rest of the class.

There are two parts to this exercise:

Day One
Interviews. Each dyad will have 15 to 20 minutes to have a conversation, during which time you will find out the things you'll be saying in the introduction of your partner. You might include such things as family and cultural background, places where the person has lived, jobs, likes, dislikes, hobbies, etc. In addition, you might include the answer to one question that everyone in the class will respond to. Here are some possibilities: "What is one important thing that has happened to this person in the past?" Or, "What is one thing that might make this person different from anyone else in the class?" **Take notes** so you don't forget anything.

Day Two

Introductions. Sign up for your speaking order so there are no awkward pauses while we wait for a dyad to volunteer. The partners in the dyad go to the front of the room together for the introductions. (Remember, there is safety in numbers!) Decide beforehand which partner will speak first and which partner will speak second. Each partner may speak for one to two minutes. If either partner wishes to use note cards, s/he may do so, but just to glance at -- not to read word-for-word.

FOUR BASIC INTERPERSONAL COMMUNICATION SKILLS

SPEAKER ROLE	LISTENER ROLE
Clear Sending (say what you mean and say it concretely)	*Reflective Listening* (paraphrase content)
Congruent Sending (send a negative message assertively)	*Active Listening* (paraphrase feeling plus content)

This diagram illustrates the four *basic interpersonal communication skills* that underlie all communication situations. We have prepared a series of four activities that will provide interpersonal practice sessions using these four skills. Each activity is presented in four parts:
1) A definition of a concept
2) Instructions to write an *Agenda* (which you will prepare in order to participate in the practice session)
3) A *Workshop* description which details your practice session with your partner(s)
4) A *Response Sheet* that you will complete after your practice session is completed.

The goal of good communication is "assertiveness," avoiding "passive" behavior on one end, or "aggressive" behavior on the other. All communication can be understood in terms of this continuum

PASSIVE	ASSERTIVE	AGGRESSIVE
1. Ongoing silence	1. Reflective listening	1. Arguing
2. Automatic agreement	2. Clear sending	2. Interrupting
3. Not listening	3. Focusing on the task	3. Distracting
4. No risk-taking	4. Encouraging participation	4. Wandering off the subject
		5. Fooling around
		6. Monopolizing

Reflective Listening

1.   Concentrate on the other person. Forget yourself for the moment.

2.   Get the main idea of what the person is saying.

3.   Hear something concrete in what the person is saying.

4.   Don't "block" -- that is, don't "evaluate" by:

        --judging   --agreeing

        --advising   --sympathizing

        --questioning   --kidding

        --analyzing

Clear Sending

1.   State the main idea simply and clearly.

2.   Support the main idea with concrete examples.

3.   Don't "block" -- that is, avoid:

        --interrogating

        --accusing

        --using sarcasm

Clear Sending and Reflective Listening

Flight Behaviors

        The term "flight" is a way of describing the many ways -- both conscious and unconscious -- in which people run away from (or "flee") the things they don't want to face. In other words, rather than dealing with difficult or challenging situations assertively, we often try to avoid taking responsibility by falling into various "coping" behaviors, strategies which never really succeed because they keep us from taking the appropriate risks which are necessary if we are to grow more assertive and successful, in interpersonal relationships, as well as in more formal school and work situations.

        In his book You and Me, Gerald Egan explores twelve of these flight behaviors: Boredom, Talking Outside the Relationship, Psychologizing, Playing the Director, People Who Don't "Need" Skills Training, Cynicism, Rationalizing, Silence, Humor, Lack of Directness, Low Tolerance for Conflict and Emotion, Hostility. (Egan, p. 281, Reprinted with permission.)

        People can be very creative in running away from things they don't want to face. What follows are descriptions of "flight behaviors" -- behaviors individuals exhibit when they want to avoid some responsibility, for whatever reason.

BOREDOM. Boredom, it has been said, is an insult to yourself. A bored person will usually become passive. A person who is bored sees himself or herself as a *victim* of what's happening -- and tends to put the blame "out there," saying that the interaction isn't "interesting." A bored person, then, is one who has given up taking the initiative for the relationship and is just letting things happen. When confronted, he or she gives us excuses that are a bit lifeless:

"I didn't say anything because nothing was happening."

"I just couldn't get into it."

"I couldn't seem to get started."

A bored person is a burden on the relationship. Since such a person is really not attending, he or she becomes a distraction. People will notice someone who is bored, even if they don't say anything. Eventually others will feel that they have to "deal with" this bored person.

The best way to handle boredom is to involve yourself with others in such a way that you avoid becoming bored. However, if you find that you're often bored when others are talking, you may ask yourself how motivated you are to get more deeply involved with others. You are responsible for your own boredom. Boredom is a *choice*!

TALKING OUTSIDE THE RELATIONSHIP. If you're bothered by an issue that has to do with all persons in the relationship, but you deal with it outside, you drain off energy from the relationship itself. It is better to talk about the issue with all persons involved -- and to keep all persons informed of decisions made. All members in a relationship should have an idea about what is going on with other members to the degree it affects the relationship.

Stop yourself from talking outside the relationship.

PSYCHOLOGIZING. This is done if you:
- make yourself into a helper or a counselor.
- make yourself into a client or patient.
- use a lot of psychological jargon.
- spend a lot of time looking for insights into your personality instead of examining the behaviors that form your interpersonal style.

The remedy for psychologizing is to pursue mutual sharing in relationships.

PLAYING THE DIRECTOR. This is the person who gets others very involved with what is going on, but remains personally aloof. The director moves safely into ongoing conversations but doesn't initiate them. The director asks a lot of questions, comments on what is happening in the relationship, and checks out feelings of others without getting very involved in either self-disclosure or in confrontation or immediacy.

PEOPLE WHO DON'T "NEED" SKILLS TRAINING. These people will run away from interpersonal skills training saying they already possess the skills or that they are already quite effective in interpersonal relating. All of us can use a check up from time to time. Most people will find that it is invigorating to polish skills we already possess or to discover ways to improve skills we haven't used in some time.

CYNICISM. A cynic is a person who sets himself or herself apart from others and in effect sneers at the possibility of sincerity. Cynics take a condescending attitude toward many of the dimensions of interpersonal living. They don't believe that people can really care for one another. They believe that, on the contrary, most of us are motivated only by self interest. Therefore, they tend to scoff at supposedly sincere, noble, or tender human interchanges.

RATIONALIZING. To rationalize means to substitute more acceptable explanations for our own negative behavior instead of facing the real reasons for it. We use rationalizations to put the blame for our failures anywhere else but on ourselves. Some possible rationalizations might sound like:
- I really don't know what's holding me back.
- The main difficulty is that the instructor and I don't get along.
- I'm really not the interpersonal type.
- I'm quiet because others say what I want to say -- so I say nothing.

The solution to rationalizing is confronting yourself with what you are doing so you can alter your behavior.

SILENCE. A silent person may be learning a lot from listening very well, but that person is not contributing anything to the relationship. While it is true that the quality of participation is, absolutely speaking, more important than quantity, there is still a point at which lack of quantity is damaging to the overall relationship.

HUMOR. Humor is a two-edged sword. It can be used to lighten the effect of confrontation, but it can also be used to run away from some situation that may not be comfortable. A genuinely humorous person can often get a confrontation across in a lighthearted way but still make the confrontation serious and meaningful. On the other hand, some people, when things get too tense, dissipate the tension with humor, failing to realize that a reasonable amount of tension can help keep people working toward their goals. Whenever individuals adopt humor as a consistent part of their style, it is no longer serving a useful function, and needs to be confronted.

LACK OF DIRECTNESS. There are a variety of ways in which lack of directness can become a form of flight:
- Speaking in generalities -- one common way to do this is to use substitutes for the pronoun "I," such as "one," "we," or "you."
- Asking questions instead of making statements.
- Waiting for the `right' moment to say something.
- Seldom using a person's name.
- Talking about a person rather than to that person.
- Avoid sharing hunches and perceptions.

LOW TOLERANCE FOR CONFLICT AND EMOTION. People with a low tolerance for conflict and emotion will try to drop the interaction if things get "too hot," or they will try to stop what is happening. When confrontation takes place, they engage in what has been called "red crossing" in that they rush in like Red Cross Volunteers to mend the wounds of the person being confronted and to put an end to the conflict. This is not to suggest that all conflict is good or that conflict should be stirred up for its own sake. However, research studies have shown that conflict, if faced reasonably, contributes to, rather than detracts from, growth. On the other hand, conflict that isn't allowed to surface at all will keep people from developing relationships.

To deal with conflict, one should:
- disclose what's troubling you.
- reasonably confront the other person or persons.

HOSTILITY. Hostility is one of those strong emotions that many of us fear. There was a time in the development of human-relationship training when the expression of raw hostility toward others was seen as one of the most liberating interpersonal experiences in which a person could engage. Those days, hopefully, have passed; raw hostility is now seen by most as a form of aggression rather than of assertiveness.

Any use of hostility should be examined -- not because hostility is evil in itself, and not because a certain amount of hostility isn't normal in human relationships, but because hostility may really be a cover-up for something else.

ASSIGNMENT: Flight Behavior Agenda

Although these Flight Behaviors are all very relevant to the classroom or academic speech class environment, you will find it easy to identify many of them as similar to ones you employ in everyday life.

For this agenda:

1.   Select two flight behaviors that you think you employ to one degree or another, whether at home, with friends, in a school situation, or at work.

2.   Make a brief statement for each, but be sure they start with the idea clearly stated and conclude with the **concrete example** to help explain the idea. The formula, idea plus example, summarizes in a simple, easily-remembered way the essential attributes of Clear Sending.

Here are some additional instructions for completing this agenda:

a.   Employ the language of flight that is used in this text. Try to be very precise about the particular flight behaviors you use by naming them.

b.   Make clear the source of your flight. What circumstances give rise to what feelings (anxiety, stress, fear, etc.) that generate the flight behaviors?

c.   Describe concretely the actual behavior. It doesn't help to say, "I have a problem with conflict and avoid it." That doesn't help us understand exactly how you feel and what you do. For help in clarifying feelings, consult "Feeling Words," page 53.

d.   For **one** of the two entries, write out a fairly detailed concrete example of a recent time when you have used this flight behavior (One page, typed and double-spaced). There are two examples of this Agenda on the following pages.

e.   For the other entry, just refer very briefly to a concrete example, so that you will remember it in the workshop, but you don't have to write it out, as you do for the other.

In preparing your agenda, you may find Egan's discussion of Concreteness helpful. "Concreteness means talking about clear and specific experiences happening in clear and specific situations." (Egan, p. 99) A good example is made up of three parts. First are experiences (What happens to you in interpersonal situations; what others do to you; how they react to you). Second are behaviors (What you do, concretely and specifically). Third are feelings (How you feel about yourself; how you feel about others and what they do).

31

Example Agendas: **Flight Behaviors**

- - - - - -**EXAMPLE #1:** **Please double space your original reports.**- - - - - -

LOW TOLERANCE FOR CONFLICT OR EMOTION

I flee situations where I might come into conflict with another person. Mostly, I avoid conflict with my sister, Ellen. Examples of situations I might write about happened last Christmas or two weeks ago when we went shopping together.

LACK OF DIRECTNESS

I am almost always waiting for the "right moment" to say what I want. A lot of times that "right moment" never comes. I also avoid sharing hunches and perceptions. I often find myself thinking: "I thought that was going to happen" but I had never said anything. I do this at home, school, work, and when I'm out with friends. I've done it for as long as I can remember.

In February this year, I wanted to go to my seven year old daughter's Valentine's Day party at school. I had to get time off from my own work to do this. I kept putting off asking Lisa, my supervisor, for the time off. I was waiting for the right moment when she wasn't too busy and was in a good mood. Every time I went to the office to talk to her, she was talking to someone else or on the phone. Instead of waiting for her or interrupting, I would just figure that I would talk to her later, that it wasn't a good time. I guess I was afraid to ask for something I wanted because I might not get it. If I don't ask, I can't get rejected. I think maybe I thought she might think it was a dumb reason to want time off. This went on for about a week.

Finally, on the day of the party, I waited until I went in to work to ask her if I could leave early. I told her I could come back after the party also. Two teachers had called in sick and they only had one sub, so they had no one to cover for me so I couldn't go to the party. Lisa told me that if I had let her know two days before, she could have gotten a sub for me and I could have gone. If I had just asked for the time off without waiting for the "right moment," I would have gotten what I wanted.

By Cathy Cox (Reprinted with permission.)

32

PSYCHOLOGIZING

I tend to be a helper, a counselor, and one who likes to coddle others. I find myself looking for insights into my own, as well as others' personalities, looking for reasons that I may have a certain idiosyncrasy. I try to figure out why someone might act a certain way or view things in a particular way. Were they abused as a child? Do they have some sort of mental deficiency?

An example of this flight behavior would be after having completed a Child Development class here at De Anza College. I spent the next quarter analyzing the behaviors of many children, (my own inclusive). I found myself (taking flight) trying to find the deep inner-turmoil that they might be going through when acting out a negative or seemingly aggressive behavior, instead of just staying grounded, and accepting that this might be a behavior in forming an independent or assertive style of their own.

PLAYING THE DIRECTOR

Directing; planning; strategizing; that's my job! I find myself planning parties, gatherings, or activities, and then play the "Director" or the "Monitor" of the function. I find that I steadily move from conversation to conversation agreeing with a thought or comment yet apprehensive in initiating conversation or adding content to an active dialogue. I ask many questions, (this I feel occurs as to keep the subject off of myself); I feel that I am a good listener, careful not to self-disclose much. I will purposefully move past a confrontational issue or go as far as to try to change the subject or smooth things over with light-hearted remarks, as to keep a congenial air about things. I do this with family and friends as well as with students in my Biology 10 Adjunct groups, when things in "my" space seem to become confrontational or uncomfortable.

A perfect example of this behavior happened on March 25th of this year. I have found that I am able to safely get all of my family and close friends together at my home once a year, for the celebration of my two daughters' birthdays (both born in March). I plan a party of usually 50 people; adults and children inclusive. I rent an outdoor "fun-jumper," and set up the playroom with many toys and have children's videos playing for the duration of the party. I plan appetizers and a big lunch, a cake and ice-cream dessert. This keeps things moving so that I am constantly busy, leaving little time to actually be able to sit down and converse. This year was no different than any other. I flitted around from group to group, smiling, patting backs, nodding and smiling as if to make my contribution (small and in-descript as it may be).

I don't avoid these people because I am not a caring person. I just find that I feel more comfortable as a coordinator than a communicator. There is a time however, once the gathering has ended, and I am able to sit back and reflect on the day. There is always that regret that I did not sit down and enjoy the event, the people and the whole experience. There is a period that I feel like "I missed it."

Maybe actually writing this piece, I will be able to come to terms with this issue and try to find a way to look closely at this "flight behavior" and find a balance.

By Tonie Finch (Reprinted with permission.)

33

Workshop Activity: **Flight Behavior**

The Speaker in this workshop is the person using his or her agenda to practice Clear Sending. The Listener is the person doing Reflective Listening.

The target skills for this workshop are *Clear Sending* and *Reflective Listening*. The speaker should say what he or she wants to say as clearly and concretely as possible. There are two components of Clear Sending: **First**, state an idea as concisely as possible, without digressing, meandering, or introducing irrelevancies. In short, get to the point! **Second**, amplify and clarify this idea with an example. Ideas are abstract and difficult to grasp; an example in interpersonal communication often takes the form of a brief personal experience or anecdote, which the listener can follow. Brief personal experience narrations have a ring of truth about them, and a quality of particularity, which the listener can grasp easily.

Even though we aren't ready to focus on accurate listening as a target skill (see Workshop Activity: Active Listening), the principle of "Mutuality" requires that the listener respond with basic understanding, or what we call "Reflective Listening." The skill of Reflective Listening involves saying back to the speaker what he or she said, *in your own words*, as accurately and completely as possible. Students sometimes become uneasy doing this, because it is, they think, an unnatural -- even stilted -- kind of responding. It would be if we were to employ it in ordinary conversation. But we are not practicing ordinary conversation here; we're practicing high-level communication, for use in special circumstances -- both personal and formal. Also, it is true that with no imagination, no creative use of our vocabulary, the Reflective Listening we do can be reduced to mindless parroting. That, however, is not a condemnation of the skill, but merely our lack of experience in performing it. Furthermore, hidden in the students' concern is a very real truth: Reflective Listening is difficult. Its difficulty often leads students to reject it as artificial before they are able to see the array of communication doors -- in both interpersonal and group situations -- it will open for them.

- - - - - - - - - - - - - -

Response Form: **Reflective Listening**

NAME_____

PARTNER_____

(Complete this response after you have practiced reflective listening.)

As a Reflective Listener I...

35

Mutuality

The concept of "Mutuality" is not a complicated one, but it is at the heart of interpersonal relationships at any level, because it has to do with our willingness to let other people know us, and our willingness to permit others to do the same. In other words, mutuality recognizes the fact that healthy human relationships -- whether between family members, between friends, in the work place or at school -- are *reciprocal*, not one-sided. Your willingness to be open with me encourages me to take the appropriate risk of doing the same with you. There is much "give and take" in any sound interpersonal relationship.

You may not think of mutuality as a *skill*, but it is something that can be learned and practiced. Like any skill -- whether skiing, bike riding, or public speaking -- it also requires that the learner take necessary risks. The skill of mutuality encourages risk-taking for the very reason that it is "mutual," or reciprocal: Your willingness to be open and trusting with me, encourages me to be the same with you. Central to making mutuality work are the basic skills of Clear Sending and Reflective Listening. Your ability to listen to me in an accurate and non-judgmental way encourages me to be more open with you. And, your ability to talk about yourself assertively and concretely makes it easier for me to do the same with you.

ASSIGNMENT: Mutuality Agenda

For this Agenda:

1. **Choose one question from each of the ten sections below**, and answer each of the ten questions honestly and directly. Don't puzzle too long over the answers; just be honest with yourself. (When you type out the agenda to hand in, keep your original intuitive responses.)

2. For *nine* of the ten questions you chose, write only a brief reference to a concrete experience or behavior of yours that could help explain why you answered as you did. Be sure to include the question, as well as your answer. Even a few words are sufficient, since they are only to serve as a reminder when you do the workshop.

3. For the *tenth* question (can be any of the ten you chose), actually write out the concrete example in a brief paragraph of a half-page to a page, typed and double-spaced. An example of this Agenda can be found on page 40.

Some Questions about my Interpersonal Style (Egan, p. 15, Reprinted with permission.)

1. HOW BIG A PART OF MY LIFE IS MY INTERPERSONAL LIFE?
    * How much of my day is spent relating to people?
    * Do I want to spend a lot of time with people, or do I prefer being by myself, or am I somewhere in between?
    * Do I have many friends or very few?
    * Whether many or few, do I usually spend a lot of time with my friends?
    * Is my life too crowded with people?
    * Are there too few people in my life? Do I feel lonely much of the time?
    * Do I prefer smaller gatherings or larger groups? Or do I prefer to be with just one other person most of the time?
    * Do I plan to get together with others, or do I leave getting together to chance -- if it happens, it happens?

2. **WHAT DO I WANT AND WHAT DO I NEED WHEN I SPEND TIME WITH OTHERS?**
    - What do I like in other people -- that is, what makes me choose them as friends? Is it intelligence or physical attractiveness? Is it the fact that they're good-natured and pleasant or that they have the same values as I do? Do I choose to be with people because they're important or in positions of authority?
    - Do I choose to be with people who will do what I want to do?
    - Do I choose to be with people who will take over and make decisions for the two of us?
    - *Do I just spend time with whoever happens to come along?*
    - Are the people I go around with like me or different from me? Or are they in some ways like me and in other ways different? How?
    - Do I feel that I need my friends more than they need me, or is it the opposite?
    - Do I let others know what I want from them? Do I let them know directly, or do they find out what I want in indirect ways?

3. **DO I CARE ABOUT THE PEOPLE IN MY LIFE?**
    - If I care about others, how do I show it?
    - Do others know I care about them?
    - Do I take others for granted?
    - Do I wonder at times whether I care at all?
    - Do I see myself as selfish or generous or somewhere in the middle?
    - Do others see me as self-centered? If so, how?
    - Do others care for me? How do they show it?

4. **AM I GOOD AT RELATING TO PEOPLE? WHAT ARE MY INTERPERSONAL SKILLS LIKE?**
    - Am I good at both understanding others and letting them know that I understand?
    - Do I respect others? How well do I communicate that I do respect them?
    - Am I my real self when I'm with others, or do I play games and act phony at times?
    - Am I open -- that is, willing to talk about myself -- when I'm with people who want to be intimate with me?
    - Can I confront others without trying to punish them or to play the game of "I'm right and you're wrong?"
    - Do I ever talk to others about the strengths and the weaknesses of our relationship?
    - Do I make attempts to meet new people? Does the way in which I meet new people encourage them to make further contact with me?
    - Am I an active listener -- that is, do I both listen carefully and then respond to what I've heard?
    - Do people I know come to me when they're in some kind of trouble? If they do, do they leave me feeling understood or helped?
    - Am I outgoing, a go-getter in my relationships, or do I sit back and wait for others to make the first move?

5. **DO I WANT TO BE VERY CLOSE TO SOME PEOPLE?**
    - What does closeness or intimacy mean to me? Does it mean deep conversations? Does it mean touching and being physical?
    - Do I enjoy it when others share with me whatever is important in their lives, including their secrets and their deepest feelings?
    - Do I like to share whatever is important in my life with others, including my secrets and my deepest feelings?
    - What people am I close to now?
    - Do I encourage certain others to get close to me? How do I do it?

- Does closeness frighten me a bit? If so, what is it about closeness that frightens me?
- Are there many different ways of being close to others? What are these ways? Which ways do I prefer?

6. HOW DO I HANDLE MY FEELINGS AND EMOTIONS WHEN I'M WITH OTHERS?
- Do others see me as a very feeling person, or do they see me as rather cold and controlled?
- Which emotions do I express easily to others, and which do I tend to swallow or hide?
- Is it easy for others to know what I'm feeling?
- Do I let my emotions take over and rule me when I'm with others?
- Do I try to control others by my emotions, for instance, by being moody?
- Do I think that it's all right to be emotional with others?
- How do I react when others are emotional toward me?
- Which emotions do I enjoy in others? Which ones do I fear?
- What do I do when others keep their emotions locked up inside themselves?

7. HOW DO I ACT WHEN I FEEL THAT I'M BEING REJECTED BY SOMEONE?
- Does feeling left out and lonely play much of a part in my life?
- If I feel rejected, how do I try to handle my feelings?
- Do I sometimes avoid trying to get to know someone or joining a group of people because I'm afraid that I will be rejected?
- Can other people scare me easily?
- Have I ever really been let down or rejected by someone?
- How easily am I hurt, and what do I do when I get hurt?
- Do I ignore or reject others who might want to get closer to me?
- What do I do when others want to get closer to me and I don't want them to?

8. DO I WANT A LOT OF GIVE-AND-TAKE IN MY RELATIONSHIPS WITH OTHERS?
- Do I play games with others, or do I prefer to be straightforward and direct with them? Do people play games with me?
- Do I like to control others, to get them to do things my way? Do I let others control me? Do I give in to others much of the time?
- What do I ask of my friends? What do my friends ask of me?
- Are there ways in which my friendships or my other relationships are one-sided?
- Am I willing to compromise -- that is -- to work out with another person what would be best for both of us?
- Do I think that it's all right for others to influence me and for me to influence others, within reasonable limits?
- Do I expect to be treated as an equal when I'm with others? Do I want to treat others, especially my friends, as equals?
- Do I feel responsible for what happens in my relationships with others, or do I just let things "take their course"?

9. HOW DO I GET ALONG IN MY WORK AND SCHOOL RELATIONSHIPS?
- How do I relate to people in authority?
- At school or at work, do I treat people as people, or do I see them as just other workers or just other students?
- Am I so personal at school or at work that I don't get my work done?

10. WHAT ARE MY MAIN INTERPERSONAL VALUES?
- Do I want to grow in my interpersonal life and relate better to others?

- Am I willing to work, to risk myself, to put myself on the line with others in order to get involved in a richer interpersonal life?
- Am I willing to allow others to be themselves?
- Is it important for me to be myself when I'm with others?
- In what ways am I too cautious or too careful in relating to others? What are my fears?
- Do I get along with people who have opinions and views and ways of acting that are different from mine?
- Do I have any prejudices toward other people?
- How straight or rigid or unbending am I in my relationships with others?
- Do I share my values with others?
- Do I put so much emphasis on interpersonal relationships (for instance, my friendships) that they interfere with my work or with my other involvements in life?

- - - - - -

Example Agenda: **Mutuality**

Some Questions about my Interpersonal Style   **Include (your example) in parentheses.**

1. Whether many or few, do I usually spend a lot of time with my friends?
   No, I really do not spend as much time as I would like to with my friends. (Carolyn)

2. Are the people I go around with like me or different from me? Or are they in some ways like me and in other ways different? How?
   The people I go around with are like me in that they think and act in similar ways. (Gina)

3. Do I take others for granted?
   Sometimes I take others for granted, but not that often. (Husband)

4. Am I outgoing, a go-getter in my relationships, or do I sit back and wait for others to make the first move?
   I am outgoing and a go-getter, and never wait for others to make the first move as experience as taught me a lesson. (army)

5. Does closeness frighten me a bit? If so, what is it about closeness that frightens me?
   Closeness does frighten me a little because I feel very vulnerable and afraid that the other person may use it to their advantage. (child)

6. How do I react when others are emotional toward me?
   I try my best to be a good listener but sometimes I can feel awkward and stuck for words. (Prozac)

7. Does feeling left out and lonely play much of a part in my life?
   Feeling left out and lonely plays a small part in my life. (England)

8. Am I willing to compromise -- that is to work out with another person what would be best for both of us?
   Sometimes I can be quite stubborn and want things my own way. (Dad)

9. Am I so personal at school or at work that I don't get my work done?
   No, in this respect I am quite disciplined. (career)

10. Am I willing to allow others to be themselves?

 Yes, I think this is very important because I would like others to think that I can be myself. (Ray)

- - - - - -<u>EXAMPLE:</u> **Please double space your original reports.**- - - - - -

 I came to America approximately four years ago from England, a place where I had lived my whole life. This was the first time I had ever experienced real loneliness as I suddenly found myself in a foreign country with no real friends and no family. It was quite difficult at first as I was going through culture shock that left me feeling left out and longing to be with my friends in England. Although I have made lots of acquaintances I still feel lonely at times because I really do not have any `best' friends in America. My husband is the only person that is my best friend. However, he is in the army and goes away from time to time with his unit. During these times, I do occasionally feel lonely again but I have resigned myself to the fact that this is a part of my life that I have to put up with. It also makes it quite difficult when I have just started making friends from the army base and then these people have orders to work in another part of the country and therefore have to move away. However, feeling left out and lonely now plays a smaller part in my life especially since I have been going to school and meeting a few more people. I now meet people from other countries as well as England who have experienced similar feelings of loneliness.

By Jackie Cook (Reprinted with permission.)

Workshop Activity: **Mutuality**

1. You will only work in <u>dyads</u>, that is to say, with one other person at a time. If possible, however, you may also work with a different person or people later in the hour. You will improve in the skill of Mutuality as you practice with different people in the workshops.

2. Sit close to the other person in the dyad. When you are the Reflective Listener, make it clear both verbally and non-verbally that you are giving your full attention to the speaker.

3. The first speaker will choose any one of the questions from her or his agenda.

   a. Read the question right from the agenda.

   b. Read the answer just as you wrote it.

   c. Start talking about the example, to which you have either the brief reference, or, in the case of one of the ten questions, the paragraph.

4. When the speaker pauses, the listener will respond with Reflective Listening.

5. The speaker will continue talking about the example.

6. When the speaker pauses, the listener will respond with Reflective Listening.

7. Then reverse the roles.

8. Do the same with another question.

9. Continue as long as you are allowed to do so.

   TAKE YOUR TIME: Do not rush through the exercise.

Response Form: **Reflective Listening**

NAME_____

PARTNER_____

(Complete this form after completing the Workshop Activity.)

As a Reflective Listener I.....

When my partner acted as a Reflective Listener, I...

Workshop Activity: **Triad Listening**

Form groups of three members each. Take turns playing the role of Speaker, Reflective Listener, and Referee.

INSTRUCTIONS TO GROUP MEMBERS

1. You will be discussing one of the answers to the Interpersonal Questions from the previous Agenda.

2. Before you may speak, you must first summarize, in your own words, what the previous speaker said, to that speaker's satisfaction and to the satisfaction of the referee -- whether it be a question, a brief comment, or whatever.

3. If your summary is incorrect or incomplete, the referee must help to clear up the misunderstanding.

4. When someone else summarizes what you have said, do not be too easily satisfied just to continue the discussion.

INSTRUCTIONS TO REFEREE

1. Make sure group members stick to the rules.

2. Group members may not speak unless they first summarize.

3. If you, or anyone else in the group, thinks the summary is inaccurate, you must interrupt and help clear up the misunderstanding.

DISCUSSION QUESTIONS

1. Do you find reflecting difficult? Why? or Why not?

2. Does reflecting serve to clarify conversations?

3. Are there weaknesses in reflecting? Are there certain situations where it might not be appropriate? Why?

4. Is it realistic to expect people to practice reflective listening in a normal conversation?

5. What can you say to each member of the group about his/her abilities at reflective listening?

Active Listening

Acceptance of Feelings

One way we communicate acceptance, trust, and respect at a Relationship Level is by communicating acceptance of feelings as well as of facts. If we only accept facts from people, we are accepting them conditionally: "I will accept only certain parts of you; I will accept you as long as you aren't expressing feelings." People, however, come fully equipped with feelings, and that is a great part of what makes them uniquely them. The result is that when people express feelings that are not accepted, they tend to push harder, as if to prove that their feelings are justified, or to prove to themselves that it is really all right to feel the way they do. On the other hand, when feelings are accepted, they now come out less pressured, less accusatory, and less defensive. In addition, once expressed, other deeper feelings can flow in behind.

Acceptance is Different from Agreement

We have been talking about accepting feelings, but let's distinguish <u>acceptance</u> from <u>agreement</u>. You express acceptance when you say: "I understand that you feel such-and-such a way about this topic." You express agreement when you say: "You couldn't be more right. I feel that way too." In the first, you accept that the other person feels the way he does; but in agreement, you ally yourself with the other person. One way we run into problems with feelings is to assume that if someone has a different feeling from ours, one of us must be right and one of us must be wrong. But another way of looking at it is to consider that when two people react differently to the same situation, they are reacting within the rules of their own upbringing, training, experiences, and values. Because upbringing, training, experiences, and values are absolutely different for each individual, I cannot assume that just because I was horrified by an event does not mean that someone else may not be delighted -- and be perfectly consistent within his/her individual reality. <u>Yet we have a tendency to try to obliterate the other person's feelings and to try to prove that ours are correct.</u> This proves nothing: It is a fact that he feels the way he feels. The only appropriate behavior is to accept that he feels the way he feels and begin to report the way we feel. We may not have the same reactions to the same experiences, but we can begin to share enough of what is going on in us to begin to understand each other.

Ineffective Listening Responses ("Blocks")

The basis of much ineffective listening is two-fold: 1) Failure to distinguish those times when the sender is not expecting you to do anything except listen; and 2) Failure to listen long enough or with sufficient understanding of the sender's feelings to really understand the definition of the problem.
Here are twelve typical responses that listeners give which communicate to the sender that it's not acceptable to have his/her feeling:

1. **Ordering, Demanding:** "You must try..."; "You have to stop..."
   (Don't have that feeling: Have some other feeling.)

2. **Warning, Threatening:** "You had better..."; "If you don't, then..."
   (You had better not have that feeling.)

3. **Admonishing, Moralizing:** "You should..."; "It's not nice to..."
   (You're bad if you have that feeling.)

4. **Persuading, Arguing, Lecturing:** "Do you realize..?" "The facts are..."
   (Here are some facts so you won't have that feeling.)

5. **Advising, Giving Answers:** "Why don't you...?"; "Let me suggest..."
   (Here's a solution so you won't have that feeling.)

6. **Criticizing, Blaming, Disagreeing:** "You aren't thinking about this properly."
   (You're wrong if you have that feeling.)

7. **Praising, Agreeing:** "But you have done such a good job..."; "I approve of..."
   (Your feeling is subject to my approval.)

8. **Reassuring, Sympathizing:** "Don't worry..."; "You'll feel better..."
   (You don't need to have that feeling.)

9. **Interpreting, Diagnosing:** "What you need is..." "Your problem is..."
   (Here's the reason you're having this feeling.)

10. **Probing, Questioning:** "Why...?" "Who...?" "What...?" "When...?"
    (Are you really justified in having that feeling?)

11. **Diverting, Avoiding:** "We can discuss it later." "That reminds me of..."
    (Your feeling isn't worthy of discussion.)

12. **Kidding, Using Sarcasm:** "When did you read your newspaper last?"
    "My old Aunt Mary had the same..."
    (You're silly if you persist in having that feeling.)

When the sender perceives receiving one of these messages, there is a risk that the sender will become defensive and either justifies the feeling further, or closes off entirely, never allowing the listener to hear anything deeper than the "Presenting Problem."

Active Listening -- An Alternative to Ineffective Listening

An alternative to the ineffective kinds of responses is to acknowledge the other person's feeling by telling him or her what you understood them to be feeling and thinking. In Active Listening, the listener summarizes, in his own words, the content and feeling of the sender's message, and states this to the sender to confirm understanding. He puts aside his own frame of reference and looks at the world from the sender's reference point.

This is not done in a mechanical way, like a tape recorder or a parrot, but in a natural way. Except for a key word or two, perhaps, the Active Listening response is given in the listener's own words. In addition, an Active Listening response needn't always be expressed in a long statement; often, only two or three precise words are enough to let the speaker know that his or her feelings were understood and accepted. Be as natural and open as possible; avoid *formula* phrases, such as "I hear you saying that," "It sounds like...", etc.

Examples   Sender: "I've been assistant in my department for almost five years. When the department head retired last month, they passed me by and gave the job to a woman who's only been with the company for six months."

Listener: "You feel resentful that your company doesn't value you more."

—————————

Sender: "Since I've divorced my husband, I've been afraid to go out and look for a job. I don't think anyone would hire me."

Listener: "You're frightened at the thought of looking for a job after so long."

—————————

Sender: "My mother is always asking me to drive my little brothers and sisters whenever they want to go somewhere. But if I want to borrow the car to go on a date, she gives me an argument."

Listener: "You feel it's unfair to be asked to drive others around but to never be able to use the car when you want to."

The Effects of Active Listening

The benefit of Active Listening is that you have communicated acceptance of the sender's feelings. In addition, it allows you to "check out" your understanding, allowing the sender to correct you if you have misunderstood him or her. Frequently, you will find that when you employ Active Listening, people feel more comfortable in bringing problems to you and in sharing deeper problems. You may also find that when you use Active Listening, people are able to talk through their feelings and solve their own problems.

[Our experience is that Active Listening also encourages others to be open about things that *please* them, that make them happy, when they know that you will accept these feelings and not ask that they be explained, justified, or defended.]

ASSIGNMENT: Active Listening Agenda

Active Listening is a deeper and more complicated variation of Reflective Listening. You will recall that when we do Reflective Listening, we are saying back to the speaker what we heard, in order to help the speaker clarify and amplify his/her thoughts. The emphasis in Reflective Listening is on *content*, the speaker's ideas. Oftentimes, however, others in our lives express strong emotions, as well as ideas. Furthermore, because these feelings are not always expressed directly and clearly, they can be misunderstood by both the listener and the speaker. Thus, the target of Active Listening is not the words themselves, but the underlying *feelings* that the listener infers from the words.

Why do we want to focus on the feelings of the speaker? Because when those we care about -- whether family, friends, business and school associates, etc. -- have "negative" feelings about something (including behaviors of ours), they need to be able to talk about those feelings, confident that the listener will not judge, not evaluate, not preach or lecture. The ability to listen well is *a skill*, which can be learned and which needs to be continually practiced. This workshop is an opportunity to do both.

1. To do this agenda, write out a conflict with another person in your life that is **Interpersonal** in character. Try to be very concrete about who the other person or people are, where the events occur, when and why, and, in some detail, what typical events make up the problem. Try to recall specific experiences, behaviors, and feelings.

2. If there is something that you simply don't want to talk about, then don't, of course. But remember, too, that assertive self-disclosure involves appropriate risk-taking, the risk of letting another person know you.

    So choose a problem that is truly important for you. Remember that the **learner** is the Active Listener. As the person with the agenda, you are the **helper**, giving the learner an opportunity to respond to a problem about which you have real feelings.

    If you were to choose a problem that is entirely safe it would be inappropriate.

    For example, safe topics would include statements like "My carburetor has been acting up lately, and I think I'm going to have to buy a new one." . . .or, "I can't decide on what area of study I want to major in."

    We don't mean to suggest that these aren't real concerns, but if you do choose such a problem for your agenda, then the **learner** won't be able to get much out of the Active Listening workshop, because the person with the agenda won't have a real emotional investment in the problem, and there won't be strong feelings for the Active Listener to respond to.

    Be sure to choose a conflict with another person or persons. For example, shyness may be a huge problem for you but it is not appropriate for use in writing this agenda since the problem presented needs to be a conflict with another person.

3. How long should this agenda be? Between a page to a page-and-a-half, typed and double-spaced, should be enough. An example of this Agenda can be found on the following page.

Example Agenda: **Active Listening**

- - - - - -**EXAMPLE:** **Please double space your original reports.**- - - - - -

A personal problem I am facing right now is a very difficult problem I am facing on my own. It has to do with my parents. The problem starts with my parents not knowing how to speak any English. Since they don't speak any English I basically take care of everything for them. It takes most of my time taking care of my grandparents alone. I have SSI to take care of for them, I have their MediCal to take care of, and when they are ill I have to take them to the doctors appointments and hospital appointments. I basically take care of anything that has to do with any English communication.

As a full time student and a part-time worker, this is already a full schedule for me each day. And, I'm so tired and worn out each day and they, my parents, have errands of their own for me to do, along with things for my grandparents. It would be easier if my brother would help me out a little, but he is living his own life taking care of a business of his own. Though he should have time for his family no matter what, he seems to be the last person to show up for any family crisis.

I honestly don't mind doing these things for my family, because if I, as the daughter and granddaughter, don't take care of my family, who will? But, one thing I ask of my parents is to give me some freedom. After taking care of them during the week, I don't even have any time to spend with my friends or boyfriend. Since I'm busy devoting my life during the week taking care of my family I want the weekend for myself. I don't think this is "too much" to ask of my parents but in their book it seems to be "too much" to ask. They get so angry when I come home a little late on the weekend. My dad will say things like, "Don't you ever stay home!" or "Do you have to go out every single day!" This is exactly what he said to me this weekend when I stayed out a little late.

My grandmother was in the hospital for a week and I went through hell taking care of her at the hospital. She also doesn't speak any English so someone had to be by her side to translate anything that was asked of her to do. And since my brother had his job, I had to be the one to be by her side. By the end of the week from running back and forth to the hospital to school, and to work, and home, then back to the hospital I thought I was going to literally collapse. And finally, when my grandmother returned home, I thought I had some time to spend with my boyfriend, but my dad was angry that I was coming home a little late.

I don't know how much longer I can take this. I feel that if I do a little bit of giving so should they, but it seems as if they are only doing the taking. I never ask them for an allowance, or a car, or for any craved food, or any clothes. I provide all of these on my own. I never asked my parents for anything. And I feel it's not been fair for them to not grant me this one favor of freedom. But on the other hand, I feel terrible that I'm even complaining about doing something I should already be doing for my parents. I guess I feel a little selfish. Don't get me wrong, I love my family more than my life itself and I know they love me too. But I can't help getting a little frustrated sometimes. Though I'm sure they get very frustrated not being able to speak any English.

By Jenny Yu (Reprinted with permission.)

Workshop Activity: **Active Listening**

In the workshop, you won't actually read the agenda, but will simply talk about it to one other person, who will respond by Active Listening.

- - - - - - - -

Response Form: **Active Listening**

NAME_____

PARTNER_____

(Complete this form after practicing Active Listening)

As an Active Listener I...

Feeling Words

In order for us to become high-level communicators in interpersonal relationships, we must become more aware of feelings in ourselves and others, acquire communication know-how, and be assertive in using the skills we learn. This entire process presupposes that we have a ready vocabulary of feeling words. What good is awareness of a feeling without the ability to express it in words and so communicate it accurately to another person? Our language is rich in words to describe subtle shades of feelings. Partly because our culture does not encourage talking about feelings, we grow up all too often virtually illiterate with respect to this vocabulary. We may go days on end without thinking about feelings and emotions; this is only natural. But when the time comes for awareness, communication skills, and assertiveness in an interpersonal situation, we must be prepared to use the language that the situation demands. One of our tasks in this class, therefore, is to enlarge our vocabulary, and to make the use of feeling words instant and accurate. You will notice that the words in the left column describe "OK" feelings; those in the right column, "Not-OK" feelings. Some of the words may not feel right for you -- may not seem to fit your interpersonal style. Scratch them and add others. By the end of the course, you should have added many words to both columns and be using these words easily and quickly in practicing the communication skills you have learned.

Happy	Frightened
Contented	Upset
Joyful	Frustrated
Enthusiastic	Worried
Glad	Annoyed
Pleased	Hurt
Cheerful	Overwhelmed
Encouraged	Dissatisfied
Light hearted	Stymied
Lively	Discouraged
Merry	Melancholy
Confident	Lonely
Elated	Resentful
Optimistic	Depressed
Accepted	Alienated
Valued	Rejected

Congruent Sending

Congruent Sending might be seen as the other side of the coin from Active Listening. Both are basic communication skills whose purpose is to keep the lines of communication open when "negative" feelings are being expressed. Neither is a "quick cure" for a problem. No such cure exists, of course. Instead, Active Listening and Congruent Sending are skills that encourage people to act assertively, rather than falling into passive or aggressive modes of behavior. Active Listening is a "listening" skill which encourages others to take the risk of assertively expressing strong feelings to you.

Congruent Sending is a "sending" skill which allows one to honestly communicate negative feelings without provoking a defensive or hostile response from the other person. This is done by "owning the problem," accurately describing the feeling that you have, and giving an objective description of the other person's behavior which evokes the feeling. Maybe now is the time to make this important point: Congruent Sending is not a way of "telling someone off." That would be "aggressive," rather than "assertive," behavior. We tell someone off when we want to "distance" ourselves from someone, or even end a relationship all together. Don't confuse Congruent Sending with "letting it all hang out," or "spilling your guts." Instead, we send a "Congruent Message" when we want to improve an important relationship; it is a way of growing closer, of trying to address a problem which is, in fact, interfering with our ability to be close to someone we love, care about, work or attend school with, live near, etc.

One distinction which it is important to be clear about is that the conflict between you and the other person is over "**needs**," and not "**values**." A "conflict of needs" is one in which another person's behavior interferes with what we perceive to be a legitimate need of our own. A "conflict of values" is over different beliefs or likes, and, though the difference may be an important one, it is not appropriate to try to resolve it through communication skills. If a daughter likes a kind of music which her mother finds ugly, that is a "value conflict"; the mother can express her opinion, but the daughter's taste in music doesn't interfere with any **need** of the mother's. But if the daughter plays the music at a loud volume when her mother wants to read, or talk with a neighbor, or sleep, then that may well be a "need conflict" and appropriate for Congruent Sending.

Suppose you have a friend, someone you've known and liked for years, and this person has the habit of occasionally borrowing your textbooks, rather than buying his own. Usually it's not a problem; but on a few occasions, he's neglected to get the book back to you when he said he would. Last Friday, you were supposed to meet in the Campus Center after your last class, so he could get your textbook back to you, but he forgot to show up. You didn't get the book until Sunday evening, when it was too late to do much studying. This situation, which has happened before a number of times, clearly represents a "conflict of needs."

Typical Ways of Sending: The three most typical ways of sending feelings (sending a solution, evaluating, and indirect messages) run some risks of creating defensiveness or resistance.

1. Sending a Solution: Rather than telling the other person what you are feeling, you tell them what you want done about it. This could be an order, suggestion, piece of advice, etc.

Example:

Congruent Message: "I really get annoyed when you borrow my book and don't return it."

Solution Message: "Don't ever borrow my book again." or: "Why don't you get your own book?"

The risks are as follows:

a) Sending a solution implies a power differential -- someone is higher, someone is lower -- and *people resist the use of power* even when they agree with the solution.

b) Sending a solution defines the problem poorly. Once you give a solution, *enforcing the solution* becomes the problem, whether or not the solution solves the initial problem.

c) Sending a solution communicates a *lack of trust*. Implied in sending the solution is the communication that you don't expect the other person to be able to figure out the solution.

2. Evaluating: Another frequent method of sending is to evaluate, blame, or judge the other person.

Example:

Congruent Message: "I really get annoyed when you borrow my book and don't return it."

Evaluation Message: "You're rude and selfish about borrowing things." or "You're certainly inconsiderate."

The risks are as follows:

a) *People become defensive* when you judge or evaluate them.

b) The Judge or Evaluator is in a power position -- people may *resent* your "one up" position.

c) People resent being interpreted and judged by your standards.

3. Indirect Messages: Indirect messages are messages which contain no direct expression of the Sender's feelings, although frequently the feelings are implied by voice tone, emphasis, sarcasm. They include "cuts," questions, "cloaked" messages, denials.

Example:

Congruent Message: "I really get annoyed when you borrow my book and don't return it."

Indirect Message: "Got any extra copies?" or: "If people in this class would be more thoughtful, it sure would make it a nicer place to study."

The risks are as follows:

a) *The message may never get through.* You may be so indirect that the other person doesn't understand you have a problem.

b) What does get through tends to be *unclear* and *undefined* negative feeling. One result of this is that it is difficult to solve the problem. It is too *ambiguous*.

c) Ambiguous negative feeling tends to be understood as a generalized rejection rather than a specific reaction. (If I know you are upset, but I'm not quite sure why, I will tend to believe "He doesn't like me," rather than "He's upset because I didn't return his book.") Sometimes this may result in the Listener totally isolating the Sender or even launching a massive counter-attack to the imagined rejection.

An Alternative: Congruent Sending. The alternative to these methods can be called Congruent Sending. The term "Congruent" comes from the fact that in a Congruent Message the message and the "code" coincide, fit, are congruent.

This "congruence" consists of **three** parts:

1. Sending feelings instead of evaluations or solutions.

2. Ownership of feelings.

3. Describing, rather than evaluating, behavior.

1. Sending Feelings Instead of Evaluations or Solutions:
   In Active Listening we attempted to state for the sender the feelings we understood to be implied in his statement. When we are sending, rather than rely on the other person to understand all the implications, we indicate our feelings directly. We tell the other person what is really going on in us. A congruent message typically contains a *feeling word*. When we are hurt, annoyed, pleased, frustrated, happy, we say that we are hurt, annoyed, pleased, frustrated, happy.

2. Ownership of Feelings:
   In order to be congruent, the sender must "own" his feelings. By "ownership" we mean that the sender does not blame or accuse people for his feelings but takes responsibility for his own feelings. First attempts to communicate feelings usually come out, "You hurt me when you said that." This is a "you" message, a feeling message made blaming and accusing by virtue of the pronoun "you," which indicates that the other person is responsible for your feeling. **The Congruent Message is usually an "I" message,** such as, "I felt hurt when you said that."

3. Describing, Rather than Evaluating, Behavior:
   The behavioral description is the statement which indicates the behavior about which you have a feeling. It is very easy to confuse behavioral description with an evaluation.

Example:

"I really get annoyed <u>when you borrow my book and don't return it</u>."
(The underlined part describes behavior.)

"I really get annoyed <u>when you're so inconsiderate</u>."
(The underlined part is an evaluation, with all the risks involved in sending evaluations. Though it begins like a Congruent Message, it is really a disguised "You Message," which degenerates into "blaming.")

The Behavioral Description specifies the other person's behavior without judging it. It also indicates the specific behavior about which you have feelings, so that the Listener understands which behaviors to modify if he wants you to feel differently.

A Formula for Congruent Sending

A simple formula for Congruent Sending is:

"I'm"   +   feeling word   +   behavioral description

OWNERSHIP   +   SENDING FEELINGS   +   DESCRIBING, NOT JUDGING

Effects of Congruent Sending

Congruent Sending encourages you to be a great deal more open and direct with your feelings. The result is that people learn to trust you -- they do not have to guess at what you are thinking and feeling. Your openness also encourages openness in others. In addition, by owning your feelings and avoiding judging, you can minimize defensiveness while dealing directly with problems.

ASSIGNMENT: Congruent Sending Agenda

To do this agenda:

1.   Write out a problem situation that is **Interpersonal** in character.

2.   Explain clearly who the other person is that is involved in the problem.

3.   Specify the nature of the problem -- that is -- what behaviors can you describe that characterize this other person and which behaviors tangibly interfere with your fulfilling your needs. Why is it a "conflict of needs," and not of "values"? Say why you "own the problem."

4.   Just describe the conflict as concretely as you can. (About a page-and-a-half typed.) Don't give solutions to the conflict; just present the problem. If you are to get the most from the workshop, choose a situation which is still unresolved, not one from the past. Two examples of this Agenda can be found starting below.

Example Agendas: Congruent Sending

- - - - - -**EXAMPLE #1: Please double space your original reports.**- - - - - -

My Neighbor Sue (not her real name) never lets me finish a sentence without interrupting me to either negate my thought, or "one-up" me. We are together every morning at the "bus-stop" where our children all gather. I try to make a concerted effort to ask, "how are you?" She doesn't say much, until I might bring up how my husband cooked dinner the night before, as I had a paper to write, and she immediately will start in on how her husband "make the best zucchini bread over the weekend." I just don't like feeling as though we are in a competition. She will ask my plans for the day, and when I mention that my oldest daughter has gymnastics or that we are going shopping later--before I can finish, her hand flies up and she just has-to-tell-me, how she had been shopping all day (the day before) and couldn't find a thing she was looking for. "Can you believe it? We spend all this money on a new day-bed, and no one has the bedding to do with it." I find myself not even listening after awhile. I am fearful of eye contact, for fear she may read my next thoughts and beat me to them. Sue came by yesterday, late in the afternoon, to see if my youngest daughter wanted to play for a half-hour with her son, while she washed her car. I was so excited about a new dish I was fixing and said to her, "How does this sound for dinner?" and before I could get the next word out, she said "OH! We just finished the BEST filet mignon we have ever had!" I find myself feeling so defeated when we converse. She minimizes my contribution to her advantage. I feel as though she is denying my needs for individuality and originality when we are together.

A character description of Sue:
--She is 37 years old, married and a mother of two boys. Whether the conversation is of a positive nature or negative, her husband, or her boys have done it, "so much better" or "so much worse."
--She is always trying to "one-up" or "out-do" others in conversation. Bigger and Better.
--Sue is always telling others how "she would have done it this way," or "well, when we put in our new bathroom, we only used solid Oak for the cabinets. Why would you use other cheap and low-quality materials?"
--Sue always waves her hand at the person who is talking, as if to stop them in their tracks or in the middle of a sentence -- to be able to interject her thoughts or feelings on the subject matter. "NO, no, no, Listen to this....." is how she usually begins her dissertation.
--If one is planning a vacation or outing, Sue has, "been there, done that," and begins her lead-in on "her" upcoming plans before one can even collect their thoughts to realize what has just happened.
--Sue's specialties: car shopping, appliance shopping, home improvement, food preparation, child delivery or rearing, medicinal information, movies, travel information. She has done it all!!! "You know, it's just not something that sparks an interest in MOST people."

By Tonie Finch (Reprinted with permission.)

- - - - - -**EXAMPLE #2: Please double space your original reports.**- - - - - -

I am taking a night class, and one of my friends is in the same class. Because I don't have a car, she offered to pick me up and take me home on these days. My problem is, she comes to pick me up late two out of three times, and as a result we both come to class late usually five to ten minutes. I miss part of the lecture, and have trouble keeping up with my notes. My only other possibility to get to class is either ride my bike or walk, but during this time of the year I'm very much likely to arrive in class wet, so I need a ride to school.

My friend lives about ten minutes away from my home. From my place it takes about five minutes to get to school, but I'm not on her usual route to school. She works on class days until four. Class doesn't start until five and her workplace is only five minutes away from her home. She is married, has no children, but a huge dog which needs to be walked quite often. She apologizes every time she's late to pick me up and presents a good reason, but we still arrive to class late. Her reasons are usually: no gas in the car and she had to stop at the gas station, or she had to take a shower, or the dog needed to be walked and her husband wasn't there to do it, or she was working late. Her reasons are understandable, but it doesn't help me to get to class on time.

By Renate Deutsch (Reprinted with permission.)

Workshop Activity: **Congruent Sending**

In the workshop, you will work with one other person, who will "role-play" the person with whom you are having the conflict that you describe in your agenda. It doesn't matter if the role-player is not the same age or sex as the actual person; if you make an honest effort to "get into" the part, you will discover that feelings are universal, transcending differences of sex, age, race, ethnic background, etc. (This discovery is an additional benefit of this exercise.) There are three parts to the workshop:

1. Read the agenda aloud, so that the other person knows who he or she is role-playing. Then just put the agenda away, you won't be needing it any more for the workshop.

2. Get the feeling of sending the wrong kinds of messages. (The feeling should be all too familiar!)
   a) First send a "Solution Message." The role-player should respond just like you would in a real life situation if someone talked to you like that. Let the conversation go on for awhile. Does it seem familiar?
   b) Then do the same for the "Evaluation Message" and the "Indirect Message." For all three, let the conversation go on for a while. It's useful to see why these "non-congruent" messages, though they seem very "natural," are also not very successful.

3. Now send a Congruent Message. It may take you a while to construct a good one, because most of us simply aren't used to doing it. When you send the Congruent Message, the role-player should respond in whatever way seems appropriate to this message. Is there any difference from the way you felt with the first three? Hopefully, even though you might still feel defensive, you will also feel better able to respond assertively, rather than passively or aggressively. Remember, the skill of Congruent Sending doesn't pretend to "solve" a problem; its goal is simply to keep communication open and constructive while you try to deal with the problem. Because the person with whom you are having the conflict will probably respond defensively even though you communicated as skillfully as you could, be prepared to repeat the Congruent Message two, three, or four times using different words as much as possible. Try to resist becoming frustrated and falling into passive or aggressive modes.

A word about *anger* as a "feeling word." It's really impossible to send a Congruent Message when you're feeling very angry. Even though the words will be right, the other person will only get the non-verbal "attacking" message. Wait until some later time, when your anger has subsided, to send the Congruent Message. And rather than saying, "I feel angry," try to discover what emotion preceded the anger. That is the "feeling word" you want to send. Anger is always preceded by another emotion such as fear, frustration, rejection, guilt, loneliness, resentment, etc. Select a more specific "feeling word" than *anger* to describe your emotion.

- - - - - - - -

Response Form: **Congruent Sending**

NAME_____

PARTNER_____

(Complete this form after doing the Congruent Sending Activity.)

As a Congruent Sender I...

PRACTICING INTERPERSONAL COMMUNICATION SKILLS

Instructions for a Long Term Project

We believe that practicing interpersonal communication skills is a private experience. We also realize that the interpersonal skill you may wish to practice may not be the skill your classmate wishes to practice. In order to facilitate your practice of interpersonal communication skills, we are including a List of Skills and Possible Learning Plans. These Skills and Learning Plans were developed by Dr. Paul Friedman, University of Kansas, Communication Studies Department. (Reprinted with permission.) These two lists will be the basis for your practice sessions.

Throughout the course you will have the opportunity to practice a number of interpersonal skills that you select from the following List of Skills. You should practice the skill more than once, if possible, during the time allotted and then select a learning plan from the Possible Learning Plans in order to reflect on the results of your practice sessions.

NOTE: When selecting a skill for practice, take a risk to practice something in the "here and now" rather than something from your past. The point of the activity is to practice a skill that you can then discuss in this class.

At assigned times throughout the course, you will report the results of your practice sessions to the members of your Interpersonal Communication Skills Group. This group will remain together for the entire time of the course. The specific dates for these reports are noted on your calendar for the class. On each of these days you will need to come prepared:

1. To discuss your interpersonal skill practice sessions, the results, and your learning plan application with the members of your group, and

2. To turn in a written report which meets the following criteria:
    (Four examples can be found starting on page 67.)

    a. List the Skill number and quote the specific segments of the Skill you have practiced.

    b. List the Learning Plan number and quote the specifics of the Plan you selected for application.

    c. DESCRIPTION OF SKILL PRACTICE SESSIONS. Write a minimum of one paragraph (at least 200 words) to specifically describe how you practiced the skill and indicate the outcome of those practice sessions.

    d. APPLICATION OF LEARNING PLAN. Include the "product" of your learning plan (i.e., a short story, a game, a list of questions). There are a few cases in which the "product" may not be in written form -- so you would include the "product" along with a written explanation. *The Learning Plan application is in addition to the Description reported in Item c. above and is different from the 200-word description.*

List of Interpersonal Skills
Face to Face Interaction (no email or other written form)

1. Initiate ideas and actions forcefully; assert yourself when you are right; feel able to give orders when the situation calls for it.

2. Meet and get to know people; overcome shyness; begin a new relationship; introduce yourself to someone you don't know; go to an event where you don't know anyone.

3. Help someone in difficulty by discussing his/her problem; encourage or support someone in personal distress; respond to a friend in trouble.

4. Resolve a conflict between two people; settle an argument; negotiate an agreement; help people see someone else's point of view.

5. Frankly criticize someone to help him/her improve behavior in some way; offer suggestions for improvement to someone who needs it.

6. Express your feelings; be genuine about showing your emotions; be regarded as an open, frank person; feel spontaneous; act freely.

7. Argue well; be able to say exactly what you mean; logically defend yourself; reason clearly; recognize fallacies in the arguments of others.

8. Convince others of the value of an idea or process; be persuasive; use many approaches in your attempts to change someone's thinking.

9. Listen carefully to others without judgment or advice; listen to others without going beyond what they are saying; be gentle, sensitive.

10. Say "no"; refuse a favor or request; reject someone's offer to be with you; if any one of these is something you really don't want to do. Be abrupt with someone when necessary.

11. Tell someone something unpleasant or sad; break bad news to someone when necessary.

12. Get a group of people outside of this class to work together; share ideas; cooperate, reach a decision; solve a problem.

13. Say what you mean and have it understood by others; encourage others to listen to your ideas.

14. Explain an idea or process to someone; give a factual report; give directions clearly so that they are easily followed.

15. Relate to people from different social groups or cultures; discuss different points of view with people of different ages, races, etc.

16. Ask someone for a favor; make a request; ask to be included in a group; ask for a date; ask for a loan, ask for personal attention.

17. Be independent; differ from others in a group; refuse to conform or go along with a group; state an unpopular opinion, if that's really how you feel.

18. Express gratitude, appreciation; thank someone for a favor or advice.

19. Be strict or stern with someone; admonish; be firm about some error or wrongdoing; reprimand someone.

20. Complain about bad treatment or service; rebel against an injustice; speak up about prejudice.

21. Be reserved, dignified, poised, sophisticated in socializing or bargaining; feel and appear unruffled, self-controlled, calm.

22. Express warmth or friendliness to someone you like; show caring, appreciation, and love to a close friend.

23. Be objective, fair-minded, impartial in a conflict situation or dispute; be regarded as honest, sincere.

24. Make conversation, chat, converse to pass the time in an informal social situation; make small talk when first meeting someone.

25. Change a stiff, false, phony conversation into a more genuine personal one; encourage someone to be more real with you, to level with you.

26. Support a good idea from someone you dislike, mistrust, or usually ignore; try to see the best in someone you don't get along with.

27. Make a good impression at an interview; be able to convey relaxation with voice, body movement, and eye contact in an interview.

28. Admit an error; give in to another's point of view; apologize when you have done something wrong.

29. Keep calm in a crisis situation; avoid becoming upset; be able to think when others are reacting emotionally; be cool and collected.

30. Share a personal problem with someone else; reveal things about yourself that you don't normally share; share a weakness or secret.

31. Conduct an interview with someone from another cultural background, religion, or sexual orientation (Include your interview questions in the Outcome section).

32. When people are gossiping about a third party who is not present, stick up for that person or say something that will get them to stop gossiping.

33. Be silent for several short periods of time; take silent strolls by yourself; turn off the car radio; pray; meditate; listen to yourself.

34. Touch people more; hug your family and friends when saying goodbye; sit close to your spouse.

35. Smile more to strangers; smile more to people at school, work, play, and church; talk into a mirror when on the telephone.

36. Spend time with an old person or a young kid in the neighborhood; just listen to the person; maybe even take them out for an ice cream.

37. Visit a different church or synagogue; talk to a minister, pastor, or rabbi from another religion or denomination.

38. Interview a family member about your cultural history regarding immigration, traditions, etc. List your Interview questions in the Outcome section.

39. Your choice. Write your own skill, practice it and report to your group. (Check with your instructor before selecting #39.)

Possible Learning Plans

INTROSPECTION

1. Draw anything that comes to mind about this skill. Write a paragraph explaining how you felt about your drawing.
2. Write an essay about this skill.
3. Describe and analyze one other experience where this skill was involved or needed in your life.

SYMBOLIZATION

4. Write a play, poem, construct a collage, or take some photographs inspired by your thoughts about this skill. Write a paragraph to explain your choice.
5. Write a song about this skill and play it for the group. Discuss the results of your performance.
6. Discuss how this skill is portrayed in films, television, or stage.

PRACTICE

7. Select a scene from a play or movie where this skill is being used. Read the line out loud for someone. Describe how you felt about doing this activity.
8. Role-play the skill with a friend five different times. Discuss your feelings and any improvement you noticed.
9. Plan and practice another specific instance outside of class where you will use this skill. Do it. Discuss how it went.

FEEDBACK

10. Ask a person you really trust their opinion of your performance of this skill. Discuss it in relation to your opinion of what was said.
11. List some questions you have regarding this skill. Put them into a questionnaire and ask (or interview) 5 others for their answers to the questions. Discuss their responses.
12. Describe a problem situation in which this skill is involved (like a "Dear Abby" letter) and ask 5 people for a response. Discuss what they said and your response to their statements.

OBSERVATION

13. Try to observe this skill being used in real life. Record and summarize your observations.
14. Find a scene in a favorite play, book, or movie in which this skill is used, and analyze it thoroughly.
15. Conduct an experiment to answer a question you have about this skill. Summarize and discuss the results.
16. Conduct an interview with someone who practices this skill. Summarize and discuss the interview.

TEACHING

17. Create a learning experience by which you could teach this skill to others. Do it. Discuss the experience and the results.
18. Invent a game that stresses this skill. Describe the game.
19. Invent a test that measures this skill. See if people that are good at this skill really score higher than others -- this will show you created a good test. Discuss the test and the results.

BOOKS

20. Critically review one book that deals with this skill.
21. Think of a famous person who used this skill. Read a biography of him or her and describe how they developed this skill.

22. Look up all the quotations you can on this skill. Select the best three and discuss each in your own words.
23. Relate this skill to your future work or profession. Ask someone already in the field to suggest readings in this skill area. Discuss the findings of your readings.

YOUR CHOICE
24. Write your own learning plan, experience it, and share it with your group. (Check with your instructor before selecting #24.)

Examples: **Skill Practice Reports**

- - - - -**EXAMPLE #1:** **Please double space your original reports.**- - - - -

Skill #5:   Frankly criticize someone to help him/her improve behavior in some way; offer suggestions for improvement to someone who needs it.

Learning Plan #22:   Look up all the quotations you can on this skill. Select the best three and discuss each in your own words.

OUTCOME OF SKILL PRACTICE SESSIONS

For the past week Sam has hurt my feelings and made me feel bad every time I talk to him. I kept taking it and taking it until I snapped. I asked other people that know Sam if it was just me or if he had changed. Everyone I talked to said they had noticed something as well. Sam was getting a large ego and driving everyone crazy. No one wanted to be around him anymore. Sam was not aware of this yet, but very soon he would be if no one said something to him. Once I had enough and "snapped", I decided I was the one to confront Sam.

Sam and I have a special relationship. We were going out about three months ago, but are very different people so things didn't work out. We stayed friends though. I've always made sure Sam knows I'm here for him because I know he doesn't think that about many people. I called Sam up and plainly told him that we needed to talk. I explained that my feelings had been hurt lately and that needed to stop. I started speaking to him in rather blunt terms and that got his attention. I asked him if we could meet to talk.

My next step was to explain to him that I was telling him some things because I care about him. I told him that he was alienating his friends and if he kept that up he would lose them. I gave him specific examples about his alienation. I tried to convince him that his friends, including myself, wanted the "old Sam" back. Everything I said was in plain terms and said sincerely. For each example I had given him, I then gave him a suggestion for change.

Sam listened to everything I said, but wasn't too receptive about following it. He said he wasn't sure if he wanted to change. I told him I couldn't ask for anything else. I hadn't talked to Sam since the conversations I just described, until he called this morning. He said he thought about what I said and apologized for being a jerk. He thanked me for telling him what I did. After some thought, he said he could see what I was talking about.

APPLICATION OF LEARNING PLAN

"The rule in carving holds good as to criticism; never cut with a knife what you can cut with a spoon." Charles Buxton

This quote basically told me that when you must criticize someone the most effective way is to stay away from undo harshness. You need to try and get your message through gently. This way you won't hurt the person's feelings. If the other person gets hurt, they will be less likely to listen.

"Advice is like snow; the softer the longer it dwells upon, and the deeper it sinks into the mind." Samuel Taylor Coleridge

This quote is saying something similar to the first one. When people are forced to hear things that they don't want to, they tend to tune out what they'd rather not hear. If you can tell someone something they don't want to hear without offending them or hurting their feelings, what you say to them will be listened to and sink in deeper.

"Advice is seldom welcome, and those who need it most, like it least." Lord Chesterfield

Most people don't like or appreciate advice that is not asked for. People who need this unasked for advice don't like it. People who most need advice don't think they do.

By Amy Buckingham (Reprinted with permission.)

Skill #22:   Express warmth or friendliness to someone you like; show caring, appreciation, and love to
                  a close friend.

Learning Plan #21:   Think of a famous person who used this skill. Read a biography of him or her and
                          describe how they developed this skill.

OUTCOME OF SKILL PRACTICE SESSIONS

I am a generous person. I have a lot of friends since I possess an easy-going personality. Jane, one of my best friends, lives by herself. One day, she felt sick and I asked her if she needed my company to consult the doctor. The doctor advised her to stay in the hospital for a better and longer observation. When Jane was in the hospital for a week, I went through it with her by taking care of her at the hospital. I kept running back and forth to the hospital, to school, to work, and to home. Jane did not want to eat anything from the hospital, so I usually brought some food for her to stimulate her appetite. Moreover, I spent a lot of time with her playing games and reading books because she felt lonely. Although I was very tired of taking care of Jane, I still feel happy and willing to show my love and care for her.

On the next week, I received a beautiful thank you card from Jane. Besides, she wrote in her own words to show how she appreciates my help and care and how she values our friendship. I believe Jane is a great friend to me in my life.

APPLICATION OF LEARNING PLAN

Mother Teresa of Calcutta (1910-1997), Albanian-born Roman Catholic nun. Originally named Agnes Gonxha Bojaxhiu, born August 26, 1910. While serving as principal of a Roman Catholic high school in Calcutta, she was moved by the presence of the sick and dying on the city's streets. She aided the poor in the world. She had set up centers to treat lepers, the blind, the disabled, the aged, and the dying -- extending her work onto five continents. Mother Teresa also organized schools and orphanages for the poor. She lived on simple food and when she traveled, she took a wardrobe of only 2 saris, clad in her distinctive white cowl trimmed with blue bands. In recognition of her efforts she received her greatest award, the Nobel Peace Prize in 1979. Mother Teresa accepted all of these awards on behalf of the poor, using any money that accompanied them to fund her centers. She died of a heart attack on September 5, 1997, at age 87, in Calcutta, India.

I really appreciate what Mother Teresa has done in her life. She helped in the hospitals with the care for sick, starving, and helpless mothers. She was touched by the endless misery which was there. She lived among the poor. She even said that she wanted to live on rice and salt, like the poor. She went in slums and the streets to talk with the poor, to help them. She helped to wash the babies, to clean their wounds. She taught poor children how to read and write, how to wash and have some hygiene. when the number of poor and sick that asked for help was increasing, the admiration for the free devotion of the sisters was growing as well. Mother Teresa went all over the world to help people, rescue children, and advise her sisters.

By Rita Ng (Reprinted with permission.)

Skill #18:   Express gratitude, appreciation; thank someone for a favor or advice.

Learning Plan #16:   Conduct an interview with someone who practices this skill. Summarize and discuss the interview.

OUTCOME OF SKILL PRACTICE SESSIONS

Too many times I have missed the opportunity to thank someone who has helped me, or have missed the opportunity to show my appreciation. Often I will be reminded at the end of a day, or after separating from the person who I appreciate. Sometimes the thought of appreciation crosses my mind, yet, for some strange reason I feel that there is going to be a special moment when I can show them how I appreciate them.

This last Thursday I decided to do an experiment. I made sure that I appreciated each person I interacted with that day. The day began with me appreciating my children for getting dressed and ready for school without a huge fuss. This made the morning a bit more cheerful. Then at the grocery store, I decided to thank the check out person for being so cheerful. It really was a nice way to start out the day. Next, I was off to the child development center on campus where my daughter goes while I attend classes. At the center I bumped into a girl named Robin who I just began a new friendship with. I told her that I was so glad we had an opportunity to go out together without our children. I told her she was fun to talk with and I looked forward to the next chance to do it again. At this point I was off to classes and became side tracked from my experiment. After school it took awhile to get back into the swing of my experiment but as soon as I had a phone call from my husband it all came back. We had an hour-long phone call and I made sure that I expressed my strong feelings of appreciation for all his support in my life. This experiment made me feel great and hopefully made others feel great as well. I think that I have a new philosophy about appreciation. It is best to give freely right when the feeling is felt.

APPLICATION OF LEARNING PLAN

I have known Linda Conroy for almost two years now. Many people ask if we are related because we have the same last name, but there is no relation. Linda is a teacher at the child development center on campus. She was my daughter Haley's first teacher. She is also a lead teacher for one of the classrooms of 2-3 year olds. As a lead teacher she is sometimes responsible for student teachers that are enrolled in that type of class. She is a wonderful person and very good at dealing with children as well as adults. When you have a child at the center it is required that you put in 3 hours a week in the classroom. Sometimes when juggling school and family, putting in hours in the classroom is the last thing you want to do. In Linda's classroom they always have a big turn out of parental help. I believe this parental support success is due to Linda's skill in delivering appreciation to the parental help in her classroom. No matter how small your help is, she always makes you feel that the work you've done is appreciated.

I decided to interview Linda on how she developed this skill of appreciation. I asked her if she made a conscious choice to behave this way? Did she learn this from her family? How has this skill affected her life? Linda stated that this skill definitely didn't come form her family. She also felt that at this point in her life she no longer had to consciously tell herself to use the skill of expressing appreciation. It just comes naturally. At the Catholic school she attended as a child, she would spend her recess time or lunchtime helping the teachers out in the classroom instead of going out to play. It made her feel really good inside to help out even though her father would tell her, "We don't pay all that money to have you help clean up in your classroom." She feels that the experience at her school influenced how she praises and shows appreciation. She knows how effective it was in motivating her and now it motivates others.

By Laura Conroy (Reprinted with permission.)

Skill #36:   Spend time with an old person or young kid in the neighborhood; just listen to the person;
                    maybe even take them out for ice cream.

Learning Plan #3:   Describe and analyze one other experience where this skill was involved or needed
                           in your life.

OUTCOME OF SKILL PRACTICE SESSIONS

In the year of 1992 my nephew was born. My oldest brother and his wife named him Isaiah Jared
Silvestre. I call him I.J. or Ijah for short. I did not actually carry I.J. until he was about three months old.
From then on I wanted to keep carrying him and never put him down. I have always volunteered to baby sit
Isaiah. I say volunteer because I do not care if I receive money for doing a job I love, and that is taking care
of my nephew. I seem to have a special bond with Isaiah. I guess that is why my oldest brother made me
one of Isaiah's Godfathers.

Last Friday I spent time with Isaiah. This was the first time in a long time that I had a chance to
spend time with Ijah. I do not know if I can just listen to him. I mean, he is only six. I mainly focused on
what this skill says about "spending time with a young kid." Anyway, I played "Nintendo" with him. Ijah
even showed me that he can read now. Isaiah's mom and I went to the library to pick up some more books
for Isaiah. At the library, he read me a short story. Sometimes he would become frustrated, but I would tell
him to keep on trying and never quit. I would help him pronounce the words he had difficulty with. Later
that day, we played basketball at my house. My mom bought Isaiah a basketball court that is for children. I
taught him how to shoot. I will tell you that he is a good shooter. My other brother and I taught Isaiah the
game of "H.O.R.S.E." By doing this, we taught our nephew a game and how to spell. I love watching
Isaiah. Every time I spend time with him, I feel that it brings out the kid in me.

APPLICATION OF LEARNING PLAN

When my mom brought my brothers and me to America, my grandma was the main person who
took care of us. As my mom became more successful in finding a better paying job, we did not need much
more from my grandma. My brothers and I grew up forgetting our native language, Tagalog, the native
language in the Philippines. This would play a large factor in our future relationship with our grandmother.
I mean my grandma could speak English, but she preferred speaking Filipino or Tagalog. Every time we
visited her, she would question in a complaining manner, "You guys don't know how to speak Tagalog?
You guys have been in America too long?" She made us feel kind of shameful. The language plays an
important role in the Filipino culture. My grandma would always ask for something in Tagalog. Even
though we could not understand, we could imply or guess what she was saying and know what she wanted.
And, plus we could always ask our mom what grandma said, then that way mom could translate for us.

As my brothers and I became older, we did not spend much time with our grandmother. We only
visited her when she was sick or when the family had a party. I wish I had spent more time with her. I wish
I took advantage of the time when she was still here. I regret this because now she is gone. She passed
away a couple of years ago. I know there was a language barrier, but I think that could have been broken
with my mom translating for us. My family really loved her. Since my mom was divorced from my father,
my brothers and I only got to see our mom's side of the family. My grandpa, my grandma's spouse, passed
away in 1985. Now, my mom has no parents and my brothers and I have no grandparents. My nephew will
not have "great" grandparents on his father's side of the family. This means when I have children, they will
not have "great" grandparents as well. The skill I needed to do was to spend more time with my grandma.
My advice is to spend time with old and young relatives; they are not going to be here forever.

By Amiel Silvestre (Reprinted with permission.)

ASSIGNMENT: Conversation Partners

Contributed by Mia Hoglund-Kettmann and Suzan Hutton-Yoshihara from their Learning Community.

Meeting #1: Intercultural Interview

You will meet someone from another culture, and will be working with the student throughout the quarter; be prepared to interview him/her. Specifically, you will need the following information. Feel free to get additional information if you have time. Be prepared to report to the class who you met and something you learned about his/her culture.

1.   Person's name (spelling and pronunciation)
2.   Where is (s)he from? How long in U.S.? How did (s)he get here? Why?
3.   What are the five most important events in this person's life?
4.   Why is this student at this college?

You may ask other questions regarding customs, beliefs, religion, values, knowledge, language, social roles, etc. if there is time. Remember this person must interview you as well. Be helpful in assisting your partner with the information (s)he needs.

Meeting #2: Cultural Idiom/Proverb Assignment

Idioms are expressions or phrases that have meanings of their own that are not apparent from the meanings of individual words. Examples of idioms in US American culture include:
Kicked the bucket = died
The lights are on but no one is home = dumb person
Beefcake = good looking, muscular man

A proverb is a brief saying; universal truth that often indicates values of a culture. For example:
"Early to bed, early to rise..."
"The apple doesn't fall...."

Pair up with your conversation partner(s) and share one idiom or proverb from your culture. Ask your partner to share an idiom from his or her culture. For each one, discuss the constructions of grammar, status, respect, meaning, significance, etc.... Be prepared to report back to our class your partner's idiom or proverb, its cultural relevance, meaning, and a context in which it is likely to be used.
    While you meet with your partner, remember to practice your assertive communication skills. Use Clear Sending (Idea + Example) whenever possible when sending messages. As a respondent, practice reflective listening as a way of validating your partner and encouraging him/her to open up to you.

Meeting #3: My Interpersonal Style

Your assignment is to practice clear sending and active listening skills by responding to the questions about your Interpersonal Style starting on page 37. This part of the assignment should be familiar to you since it is the same thing that was done for the Mutuality Agenda. Pick five questions to answer, develop your answers and give your partner time in between each answer to practice paraphrasing. Each person should have the chance to both answer questions and practice his/her listening skills. Be prepared to discuss your practice session with the class.

Meeting #4: "How unwritten rules circumscribe our lives"

After reading the article that follows, name three unwritten rules from your culture. Your partner will do the same. Discuss the article with your partner as well as the rules you identified.

The following reading is an excerpt from <u>Refining Composition Skills</u> Edited Regina L. Smalley, Mary K. Ruetten, and Joann Rishel Kozyrev.

"How Unwritten Rules Circumscribe Our Lives" By Bob Greene

Bob Greene's newspaper columns and articles are collected in Johnny Deadline Reporter: The Best of Bob Greene (1976) and American Beat (1983). In the article reprinted here, Greene writes about the power of unwritten cultural rules in our lives. As you read the essay, consider these questions:

- Are Greene's examples confirmed by your own experiences in American culture?
- Would these same examples be true in your culture?
- Can you think of additional examples of unwritten cultural rules?

1) The restaurant was almost full. A steady hum of conversation hung over the room; people spoke with each other and worked on their meals.

2) Suddenly, from a table near the center of the room, came a screaming voice:

3) "Damn it, Sylvia . . . ."

4) The man was shouting at the top of his voice. (*very loudly*) His face was reddened, and he yelled at the woman sitting opposite him for about 15 seconds. In the crowded restaurant, it seemed like an hour. All other conversation in the room stopped, and everyone looked at the man. He must have realized this, because as abruptly (*suddenly*) as he had started, he stopped; he lowered his voice and finished whatever it was he had to say in a tone the rest of us could not hear.

5) It was startling (*surprising*) precisely because it almost never happens; there are no laws against such an outburst, and with the pressures of our modern world you would almost expect to run into such a thing on a regular basis. But you don't; as a matter of fact, when I thought about it I realized that it was the first time in my life I had witnessed (*seen*) such a demonstration. In all the meals I have had in all the restaurants, I had never seen a person start screaming at the top of his lungs. (*very loudly*)

6) When you are eating among other people, you do not raise your voice (*speak loudly*); it is just an example of the unwritten rules we live by. When you consider it, you recognize that those rules probably govern our lives on a more absolute basis than the ones you could find if you looked in the law books. The customs that govern us are what make a civilization; there would be chaos (*no organization*) without them, and yet for some reason--even in the disintegrating (*falling apart*) society of 1982---we obey them.

7) How many times have you been stopped at a red light late at night? You can see in all directions; there is no one else around no headlights, no police cruiser (*police car*) idling behind you. You are tired and you are in a hurry. But you wait for the light to change. There is no one to catch you if you don't but you do it anyway. Is it for safety's sake? No; you can see that there would be no accident if you drove on. Is it to avoid getting arrested? No; you are alone. But you sit and wait.

8) At major athletic events, it is not uncommon to find 80,000 or 90,000 or 100,000 people sitting in the stands. (*grandstands, seating area in sports arena*) On the playing field are two dozen athletes; maybe fewer.

9) There are nowhere near enough security guards on hand to keep the people from getting out of their seats and walking onto the field en masse. (*all together*) But it never happens. Regardless of the emotion of the contest, the spectators stay in their places, and the athletes are safe in their part of the arena. The invisible barrier always holds.

10) In restaurants and coffee shops, people pay their checks. A simple enough concept. Yet it would be remarkable easy to wander away from a meal without paying at the end. Especially in these difficult economic times, you might expect that to become a common form of cheating. It doesn't happen very often. For whatever the unwritten rules of human conduct are, people automatically make good (*pay, do the right thing*) for their meals. They would no sooner walk out on a check than start screaming.

11) Rest rooms are marked "Men" and "Women." Often there are long lines at one or another of them, but males wait to enter their own washrooms, and women to enter theirs. In an era of sexual egalitarianism, (*equality*) you would expect impatient people to violate (*go against*) this rule on occasion; after all, there are private stalls inside, and it would be less inconvenient to use them than to wait....It just isn't done. People obey the signs.

12) Even criminals obey the signs. I once covered a murder which centered around that rule being broken. A man wanted to harm a woman--which woman apparently didn't matter. So he did the simplest thing possible. He went to a public park and walked into a rest room marked "Women"--the surest place to find what he wanted. He found it. He attacked with a knife the first woman to come in there. Her husband and young child waited outside, and the man killed her. Such a crime is not commonplace (*usual, normal*) even in a world grown accustomed to nastiness (*badness, evil*). Even the most evil elements of our society generally obey the unspoken rule: If you are not a woman, you do not go past a door marked "Women."

13) I know a man who, when he pulls his car up to a parking meter, will put change in the meter even if there is time left on it. He regards it as the right thing to do; he says he is not doing it just to extend the time remaining--even if there is sufficient time on the meter to cover whatever task he has to perform at the location, he will pay his own way. He believes that you are supposed to purchase your own time; the fellow before you purchased only his.

14) I knew another man who stole tips (*money left for waiter or bartender*) at bars. It was easy enough; when the person sitting next to this man would depart for the evening and leave some silver or a couple dollars for the bartender, this guy would wait until he thought no one was looking and then sweep the money over in front of him. The thing that made it unusual is that I never knew anyone else who even tried this; the rules of civility (*good manners*) stated that you left someone else's tip on the bar until it got to the bartender, and this man stood out because he refused to comply. (*conform, go along*)

15) There are so many rules like these---rules we all obey---that we think about them only when that rare person violates them. In the restaurant, after the man had yelled "Damn it, Sylvia" and had then completed his short tirade, (*outburst, angry speech*) there was a tentative aura (*feeling of uncertainty*) among the other diners for half an hour after it happened. They weren't sure what disturbed them about what they had witnessed; they knew, though, that it violated something very basic about the way we were supposed to behave. And it bothered them---which in itself is a hopeful sign that things, more often than not, are well.

Meeting #5: Pluralism

Your job is to teach your partner a new vocabulary word: pluralism. Define the word for your partner and give example(s). Allow time for your partner to reflect his/her understanding. When (s) he has reflected this concept to your satisfaction, ask him/her how living in a multicultural society has affected their life. Take notes. How is living here different from their native culture? Discuss how experiences differ here with respect to school, workplace, family life, gender roles, parenting. Be prepared to summarize how the two cultures differ or remain the same according to your partner's specific experience.

Progress Reports

For each meeting with your partner(s), write a brief progress report that indicates: where and when you met, day, time, location, and a summary of your progress.

ASSIGNMENT: Communication Skills Essay

The "Skills" Assignment has asked you, all term long, to improve your interpersonal skills by taking appropriate risks and then reflecting on the experience by means of the "Skill Packages." This final "Skills Essay" asks you to reflect on your communication skills.

1. What do you consider to be your **strengths** as a communicator? For purposes of this personal assessment, you can consider all aspects of communication: interpersonal, group, and public speaking.
   A. In developing your response to this question, provide **concrete examples** to help explain why you feel the way you do. The examples can come form both class activities and from other aspects of your life.
   B. Be sure to not leave the essay too abstract. Do provide concrete examples.

2. What do you consider to be **areas in which you need to improve** as a communicator? Again, as you explore this question, you can consider all aspects of communication: interpersonal, group, and public speaking.
   A. Here too, be sure to provide **concrete examples** to help explain why you feel the way you do, with examples coming form both class activities and from other aspects of your life.
   B. As you consider useful concrete examples, consider relevant behaviors and feelings.

ESSAY LENGTH: 750 - 1250 words.

NOTE: These essays will be kept in the strictest confidence. Only the instructor will read them.

BIBLIOGRAPHY

Buckingham, A. "Skills Practice Report" written in Speech 10, Collaborative Learning Class, De Anza College, Fall 1992.

Conroy, L. "Skills Practice Report" written in Speech 10, Collaborative Learning Class, De Anza College, Winter 1998.

Cook, J. "Agenda: Mutuality" written in Speech 10, Collaborative Learning Class, De Anza College, Fall 1994.

Cox, C. "Agenda: Flight Behaviors" written in Speech 10, Collaborative Learning Class, De Anza College, Spring 1993.

Deutsch, R. "Agenda: Congruent Sending" written in Speech 10, Collaborative Learning Class, De Anza College, Winter 1993.

Egan, G. 1977. You and Me. Monterey, CA: Brooks/Cole Pub. Co.

Finch, T. "Agendas: Flight Behaviors and Congruent Sending" written in Speech 10, Collaborative Learning Class, De Anza College, Spring 2000.

Fisher, B. A. 1987. Interpersonal Communication: Pragmatics of Human Relationships. New York: Random House.

Friedman, P. G. University of Kansas, Communication Studies Department, developed the Interpersonal Skills and Learning Plans used in this section of the workbook.

Greene, B. "How Unwritten Rules Circumscribe Our Lives." in Smalley, R. L., et al. Eds. 2000. Refining Composition Skills. Fifth Ed. Boston, MA. Heinle and Heinle.

Hoglund-Kettmann, M. and Hutton-Yoshihara, S. De Anza College, Cupertino, CA. "Conversation Partners Assignment."

Maslow, A. H. 1971. The Farther Reaches of Society. New York: Viking Press.

Ng, R. "Skills Practice Report" written in Speech 10, Collaborative Learning Class, De Anza College, Winter 1998.

Silvestre, A. "Skills Practice Report" written in Speech 10, Collaborative Learning Class, De Anza College, Spring 1998.

Vo, L. "Agenda: Flight Behaviors" written in Speech 10, Collaborative Learning Class, De Anza College, Fall 1994.

Yu, J. "Agenda: Active Listening" written in Speech 10, Collaborative Learning Class, De Anza College, Spring 1995.

_____. "Active Listening" and "Congruent Sending" used Copyright 1990 by permission of SYNERGY.

PART III *Small Group Communication*

INTRODUCTION

The goal of good communication is *assertiveness*, avoiding *passive* behavior on one end, or *aggressive* behavior on the other. In any discussion situation, particularly in the academic environment, there is an understandable tendency to enter in a competitive, "win/lose" state of mind (aggressive) or in a defeatist, "I can't do this. . ." state of mind (passive). But a group discussion is **not** a *collection of individual performances*, with winners and losers. Sadly, however, group communication can degenerate quickly into a situation where the *passive* drop out, the *aggressive* feel they have "won," and most everyone doesn't feel very good about the experience, not even the "winners." (That is why most people in the business environment hate to attend all the meetings that are required of them.)

Instead of an "I win/you lose" *contest* among individuals, a group discussion should be seen, as the name implies, as a *group experience*, with particular goals, requirements, and challenges. At the conclusion of a successful discussion, everyone "wins," of course, because every question asked, every idea expressed, every fact given is now the possession of <u>all</u> the members. This experience describes **high synergy.**

As with all forms of human communication, successful group communication is a matter of being aware of the necessary **skills**, and of being **assertive** enough to put these skills into practice.

Group communication involves small numbers of people, whether **informal** -- friends, family, neighbors -- or **formal** -- department meetings at work, school study or task groups, government or church committees.

What are some risks in group communication situations?

If I speak up:

> you might disagree with me.
> > you might not like me.
> > > I might have the facts wrong.
> > > > the words may not come out the way I intend.
> > > > > you might laugh at me.
> > > > > > you might be bored with what I say.
> > > > > > you might ignore me.
> > > > > > > you might think I'm silly.

Rather than take these risks, I may be **passive** and not say anything, or I may agree even when I don't. If I avoid being assertive by acting in an **aggressive** way, I may fool around, or say something "off the wall" just to get a reaction, or I may act in a hostile way toward others in the group, or I may do all the talking and monopolize the discussion. But, as with inappropriate interpersonal behavior, at either end of the continuum -- whether passive or aggressive -- it is really <u>fear</u> that is keeping me from being **assertive**.

USEFUL SKILLS FOR GROUP MEMBERS

<u>What are the skills that contribute to the success of a group discussion?</u>

1. *Listening to Others (Reflective Listening)*

   Let people know that they have been listened to and understood accurately.

   What does this accomplish?

   A. It encourages people to "think through" their ideas. (You will find that very often, after a Reflective Listening response, the speaker will elaborate on the original point, stating the idea in a more focused and complete way.)

   B. If the speaker is being misunderstood, he or she can restate the point correctly.

   C. It encourages the more reticent or timid members to be more assertive, because Reflective Listening establishes a more relaxed, supportive environment for a discussion.

   D. It encourages broader participation because Reflective Listening acknowledges the fact that some people require longer "response times" than do others.

      This phenomenon can best be shown visually:

this represents a person speaking   seconds elapsed after the person stops

*Some people find it easy to get right into the flow of a discussion as soon as the speaker has stopped. On this graphic, they would be represented by the vertical lines to the left. Others need more time before they're willing to "jump into" the discussion. These people would be represented by the lines in the middle. Others, however, find they like even more time, and would be represented by the vertical lines way to the right. If there isn't sufficient "space" between one speaker and the next, these people may well be silent for much -- perhaps all -- of the discussion. Reflective Listening allows the pace to slow down just a little bit, "buying time" for those who need it. **Where a person is on this continuum has nothing to do with the quality of the person's ideas. It's simply a matter of style.***

   <u>Two additional points:</u>

   • A Reflective Listening response doesn't necessarily have to be long. Sometimes, just a word or two is sufficient.

   • While Reflective Listening is always useful in a discussion, there are three situations where it becomes *especially* important:

      a. When someone hasn't spoken previously, or for a long time.

      b. When someone took a lot of trouble to make the point.

      c. When someone took the additional risk of saying something *personal.*

2. *Expressing Ideas Clearly and Concretely (Clear Sending)*

   A. Try to show the connection between what you're going to say and what the previous speaker has said, *whether you agree or disagree.* (This is where Reflective Listening can help.)

   B. Take the trouble to state your ideas as clearly, directly, and simply as you can.

   C. State your opinions as a **contribution to the group,** not as an *argument* to be defended to the bitter end.

   D. Try to give **concrete examples** for your ideas or opinions.

3. *Encouraging Participation of All Members*

   Look around the circle. Try to remain cognizant of the fact that a discussion is a *group* experience.

   A. Avoid dominating, or allowing others to dominate, the discussion.

   B. Avoid being passive or allowing others to be passive.

      1) If someone has been silent for a long time, you might ask him or her if they have anything they'd like to add. Sometimes you can see, from *nonverbal signals,* that they do; and your recognition was all the stimulus that was needed. (The point that this person makes may contribute in a key way to the group's understanding of the topic being discussed!)

   A suggestion: If you find it hard to be assertive in a discussion, feeling that you "don't have anything to say," then do some brief Reflective Listening occasionally, even if you have no point of your own to make at the time. This will get you into the discussion while it will also encourage others to be more assertively involved.

      2) If someone seems to be monopolizing or to be arguing aggressively (rather than *disagreeing*, which is an assertive and positive thing to do), you can tactfully, assertively (not aggressively!), suggest that someone else would like to make a point.

4. *Helping Move the Group to a Conclusion*

   Obviously, there isn't *one* conclusion to a discussion. That is why we say "to a conclusion." Nevertheless, there should be some sense of continuity to the discussion, a sense of "getting somewhere," rather than of the group's making nothing more than a series of random statements. Helping the group remain focused is an important contribution to the success of the discussion.

   A. If you see that an idea being developed relates in some way to a point made earlier in the discussion, let the group know.

   B. If there is a lull in the discussion, suggest a new issue or question that the group might consider. Try to indicate how this new direction relates to what had been discussed earlier. (Incidentally, don't be intimidated by the moments of silence that are a very natural part of any discussion.

It's only a signal that the group has exhausted the point that had been the focus of the discussion.)

Because a discussion is a *synergy* activity, different people can make different contributions to the success of the experience. Thus, it's not necessary to perform all four of these tasks, though it's commendable if you can. It's often the case, however, that people are stronger in one area than in another.

Workshop Activity: **Uncommon Commonalities**

Introduce yourselves to the other members of your group and talk amongst yourselves. Search for things that your group members have in common that are unusual or extraordinary. Your task is to discover as many "uncommon commonalities" as possible in the time allowed.

For example: All five of us are graduating in June.
                 All five of us are employed in retail sales.
                 All five of us have traveled outside of the United States.
                 All five of us carpool to school.
                 All five of us are Giants fans.

Your group may also discover some near misses, where all but one or two students share something in common.

For example: Four out of five of us are majoring in Liberal Arts.
                 Four out of five of us are adopted.
                 Three out of five of us were born in the year of the snake.
                 Three out of five of us have never seen an episode of "Survivor."

Your instructor will signal when discussion time is over, and groups will reconvene and report their results to the remainder of the class. A spokesperson can introduce the entire group or individual members may introduce themselves.

Uncommon Commonalities   Near Misses

Synergy

In her classic study of tribal societies, particularly Native American cultures of the West, <u>Patterns of Culture</u>, the American anthropologist Ruth Benedict [1887-1948] discovered that, however scientific she strove to be -- true to the spirit of the scientific objectivity appropriate to anthropological study -- the undeniable conclusion was that there were some tribes she liked and some she didn't like. Because such a subjective, "emotional," response seemed inappropriate for an anthropologist, she tried to understand her reaction by making two lists -- one of the tribes she disliked, and the other of the tribes she liked. Her approach was intuitive and subjective, rather than scientific in any formal, structured way. She made tentative lists of the qualities found in the tribes she disliked, and of the corresponding qualities in the tribes she liked. Her language in describing these qualities is personal, the kind of language we might use in ordinary conversation about people we've met. One group tended to be "anxious," the other "relaxed"; one was "surly" and "nasty," the other "friendly." One group of cultures she found to be "aggressive," the other "cooperative"; one group had "low morale," the other "high morale." One group she described as having a spirit of "hating," the other of "affection." While one group of tribes was intensely "competitive," the other tended to be "cooperative."

While it was relatively easy for Benedict to describe behavior she liked or didn't like, it was far more difficult to come up with a hypothesis for the causative factors which might explain <u>why</u> one group behaved in one way and another group in the opposite way. It wasn't, she concluded, a matter of one tribe consisting of *bad* people and another tribe of *good* people. She decided not to focus on overt behavior, but on the <u>function</u> of behavior. Perhaps the tribes *structured* themselves in ways that encouraged one kind of behavior rather than another. In her conclusions, delivered in 1941 at the *Bryn Mawr Lectures*, Ruth Benedict developed the concept of **"high synergy"** and **"low synergy"**: "Studies of the ways in which institutions in a culture either worked together and so released human energy, or else were contradictory and discrepant and so dissipated human energy." (Mead, p. 351)

She defined the terms "high synergy" and "low synergy" as follows:

High Synergy

Societies where non-aggression is conspicuous have social orders in which the individual by the same act and at the same time serves his own advantage and that of the group. Non-aggression occurs in these societies not because people are unselfish and put social obligations above personal desires, but when social arrangements make these two identical. Considered just logically, production -- whether raising yams or catching fish -- is a general benefit, and if no man-made institution distorts the fact that every harvest, every catch, adds to the village food supply, a man can be a good gardener and also be a social benefactor. He is advantaged, and his fellows are advantaged. (Benedict, quoted in Maslow, p. 202)

In other words, because a high synergy society identifies its success as coequal with its individual member's success, then it follows that the men and women of that society encourage and support each other. "Your gain is my <u>gain</u>."

Low Synergy

I shall speak of cultures with low synergy where the social structure provides for acts which are mutually opposed and counteractive, where the advantage of one individual becomes a victory over another, and the majority who are not victorious must shift as they can. (Benedict, quoted in Maslow, p. 202)

Members of a low synergy society act in a hostile, aggressive, insecure way because such behavior is needed for achievement. One's success can only come at another's expense, and the other's defeat is one of the rewards of accomplishment. "My gain is your loss."

The important point here is that the supportive, *unselfish* behavior associated with "high synergy" and the aggressive, *selfish* behavior associated with "low synergy" are the direct result of social structure, the rules of the game of any given society. People tend to act in one way or the other because that's what the cultures in which they find themselves require for "success."

Psychologist Abraham Maslow, in The Farther Reaches of Human Nature, building on Ruth Benedict's ideas, examines some manifestations of high and low synergy in primitive societies:

Syphoning vs. Funneling Wealth

Benedict concluded that secure, high-synergy societies had what she described as a `syphon' system of wealth distribution; the insecure, low-synergy cultures, instead, had `funnel' mechanisms of wealth distribution. In the funnel mechanisms, those with wealth and power employed that advantage to become wealthier and more powerful. Riches *funneled* to the already-wealthy minority. Since success in low synergy societies is measured by the accumulation and display of wealth, then the saying "The rich get richer and the poor get poorer" is not an accusation, but simply a description of the right way to play the game.

"In the secure, high-synergy societies, on the contrary, wealth tends to get spread around. It gets *syphoned off* from the high places down to the low places. It tends, one way or another, to go from rich to poor, rather than from poor to rich." (Maslow, p. 203) Maslow recalls the time when he saw such a "syphon" mechanism, during the ritual "giveaway" on the occasion of the Sun Dance ceremony of the Canadian Plains Northern Blackfoot Indians, a ceremony in which those who have accumulated wealth during the year distribute virtually all of it to the needful in their tribe. "In what way did virtue pay? The men who were formally generous in this way were the most admired, most respected, and the most loved men in the tribe." (Maslow, p. 204)

Use vs. Ownership

"We can also look at the relation of ownership to actual use of possession." (Maslow, p. 205) In low synergy societies, the function of possessions is to increase the owner's sense of well-being by provoking feelings of envy in others. "Success" in such societies necessarily means tension and hostility. In high synergy societies, Maslow observes, a man or woman who owns something finds more pleasure in its *use* by others than they do in the fact of ownership per se. He recalls that his interpreter with the Northern Blackfoot Indians, having the only automobile in the tribe, derived great pride and pleasure from lending it to anyone who needed it. "Obviously the fact that he possessed the only car in the whole society was a point of pride, of pleasure and gratification, rather than attracting to him envy, malice, and hostility." (Maslow, p. 205)

Comforting vs. Frightening Religion

"The distinction in terms of synergy also holds for religious institutions. The god or gods in the secure or high-synergy societies tend uniformly to be rather benevolent, helpful, friendly. In the insecure or low-synergy societies, on the other hand, the gods, the supernaturals were uniformly ruthless, terrifying." (Maslow, p. 205)

These contrasting styles -- high synergy and low synergy -- are expressed in all aspects of tribal life: leadership, prayer, family relationships, sexual expression, friendship, etc. "If you have a feel for this differentiation, you should be able to predict right on down the line what you would expect in these two kinds of societies." (Maslow, p. 206)

High and Low Synergy in Our Own Society

Our own society, of course, heterogeneous and complex as it is, is one of **"mixed synergy."** Some of our institutions are distinctly high synergy, some low synergy, and many have elements of both. Do the institutions in our society -- government, business, education, medicine, etc. -- operate in a high synergy or low synergy way? That makes for interesting speculation, but such broad sociological questions are not the immediate concern of this class. What *does* concern us, however, is the way small groups function. In fact, it was Abraham Maslow's purpose to apply Ruth Benedict's theory of synergy in tribal society to small group dynamics in our own society.

We all belong to many groups. Each group -- whether a family, a business department, an athletic team, a neighborhood, a school class, a church, etc. -- has its rules for success and its corresponding "synergy." Sometimes the rules which determine synergy are *explicit,* perhaps even written down. Often, the rules in a group are *implicit;* it is very likely that even the "rule-makers" are unaware of the effects of their decisions. In either case, the important thing is for you to realize that **you can help shape -- if only by the quality of your own participation -- the synergy of the groups of which you are a member.** If you are in the leadership position -- manager, coach, parent, teacher, -- then your responsibility and opportunity for helping the synergy of the group is, of course, commensurately greater. Never-the-less, all members of a group play a part in promoting group synergy, be it "high" or "low." We can look at the concept of synergy in familiar group contexts:

School Here is one example: "grading on the curve." In this case, the rules are *explicit.* Once such a system is established, with its rules for determining success, low synergy is the necessary result. If the established curve requires that there are to be 6 A's and 6 F's, 12 B's and 12 D's, and 20 C's, then my victory can only come at your expense! If you are getting a D and I am getting a B, and you come to me for help, then *by the rules of the game,* I must refuse you. Because if you move up there is a very good likelihood that I will move down. It is only natural that this system arouses feelings of suspicion, anxiety, hostility, and aggressiveness, not because we are *bad people,* but because we are playing by the rules of the group we find ourselves in.

Collaborative learning is based on a *high synergy* model. Students are given tasks that have shared goals, which invite students to respect each other as colleagues, rather than to resent each other as adversaries. These are the "rules" of the collaborative learning class. The rules are desirable, but demanding. For students to succeed in this kind of class requires awareness, assertiveness, and **communication skills.**

Family Here is another example, one where the rules are *implicit.* When a parent says to Helen, "Why can't you be more like your sister Louise? She always gets good grades and has never had one day of trouble in school," then a *low synergy* dynamic is being established, with Helen and Louise set against one another for the praise and approval that is the currency of success within the family. It would only be natural for Helen to wish for Louise's failure, once this dynamic has been established, even though that wasn't the parent's intended result. Conversely, Helen's lack of success is a "positive" for Louise, who receives steady praise as the "successful" daughter. A question then; what might be some *high synergy* ways to structure the family dynamic?

Work Students often talk of high and low synergy in work situations. They describe some restaurant managers, for example, who create a situation in which waiters and waitresses are required to compete for tips. Automatically, they become competitors, with no incentive to help each other. If this situation is aggravated by giving some waitresses the more lucrative hours and sections, then competition soon intensifies into outright hostility.

85

Students also describe restaurants in which they have worked where the synergy is high, where the employees help each other, in a friendly and relaxed atmosphere. It is valuable to consider what *rules* -- whether explicit or implicit -- have been established in these high synergy restaurants.

Coaching The *low synergy* coaches of children's athletic teams are all too familiar. The tension, the feelings of failure and resentment that permeate such teams are experienced by the children and parents alike. It is ironic that players on low synergy teams see their own teammates as "opponents"! How do these coaches encourage such low synergy group behavior? If you have ever played on such a team, you could probably come up with a number of contributing factors. To mention a few: only praising the better players; using ridicule and sarcasm as "motivators"; publicly reprimanding players; in a team sport such as soccer, praising the boy or girl who scored the goal, but not the one who passed the ball; blaming individual members when the team is doing poorly. And so on.

What about the *high synergy* coaches who help structure teams where the players are respectful of each other, where the better players help the less skilled, where spirits remain high even when the team is not doing well? What are some of the explicit or implicit rules that these coaches establish?

The important thing to realize is that you can help shape the synergy of the groups of which you are a member!

Workshop Activity: **Synergy Experience**

INSTRUCTIONS:

1)   Sit on the floor in a tight circle with your group.

2)   Distribute envelopes -- one per person.

Envelopes contain puzzle parts for forming squares. As soon as the signal is given, empty the contents of your own envelope in front of you. Start forming squares in the group -- one square per person. Each person will have a square in front of her or him. All squares will be the same size.

3)   Follow these simple **RULES**

    a) NO TALKING

    b) NO GESTURING

    c) NO NON-VERBAL COMMUNICATION OR SIGNALING

    d) NO TAKING FROM ANYONE

    e) NO MAKING A SQUARE FOR ANYONE ELSE

    f) ANY MEMBER MAY GIVE PUZZLE PIECES AWAY

Signal to the instructor when the group has completed the task.

NOTE: "Cooperative Squares" is sometimes called "Broken Squares," which can be found in:

Pfeiffer, J. W. and Jones, J. E. 1981 A Handbook of Structured Experiences for Human Relations Training.
    University Associates Inc. San Diego, CA. Vol. I. p. 25.

A Problem Solving Method

The Six-Step Problem Solving method, first developed in 1910 by John Dewey, provides groups with a High Synergy structure for decision-making, as well as for resolving conflict. Making use of basic communication skills, this method allows groups to solve problems and to reach decisions in such a way that no member of the group feels that he or she has "lost" or "given in"; and all are, therefore, committed to implementing the solution. There are six steps to this problem solving method:

I. Identifying the Problem

   A. This is a very critical step in the process. Be sure to use "Clear Sending," stating your own view honestly, assertively, and concretely.

   B. If possible, try to verbalize views that differ from your own.

   C. **Use Reflective Listening** to ensure that you understand others' views.

   D. It may take a good deal of time to define the problem or conflict accurately. **Don't be in a hurry to get to Step II.** Frequently, a problem is redefined as it is discussed and better understood.

   E. Be sure that all members accept the definition of the problem before going on to Step II. If not, you may well be trying to solve different problems!

II. Generating Possible Solutions

   A. Be willing to risk; be willing to be creative. Encourage these qualities in others by not evaluating, judging, or criticizing. Remember that, though an initial solution may be inadequate, it may stimulate someone else.

   B. **Use Reflective Listening.**

   C. Try to get a large number of solutions. If things slow down prematurely, restate the problem.

   D. Write down all solutions offered, preferably on a blackboard or chart that everyone can see.

III. Evaluating and Testing the Various Solutions

   A. This is the stage of problem solving which requires real honesty. Are there flaws in the proposed solutions? Are there reasons why a solution might not work?

   B. **State your views with Clear Sending.**

   C. **Do lots of Reflective Listening.**

   D. Be ready for the possibility that a new solution will be generated as the group evaluates a solution proposed in Step II.

E. Avoid being "side-tracked," or going off on a tangent. This tangential problem may be important, but save it for a later agenda.

IV. Deciding on a Mutually Acceptable Solution

    A. Try to reach consensus. Don't make the mistake of arguing aggressively; remember that <u>disagreeing</u> and <u>arguing</u> are two very different things. Be sure that everyone really accepts the solution.

    B. If it appears that the group is close to a decision, state the solution clearly, to be sure that all members understand what they are about to decide.

    C. Don't become impatient or discouraged at initial failure to reach a decision or solution. Keep the following in mind:

        1. Consensus takes time.

        2. Disagreement does not mean failure.

        3. If parts of the solution are acceptable to all, make that clear and focus only on the parts where there is disagreement.

        4. Be sure that there are no "hidden agendas" which are preventing agreement. (A hidden agenda is an unstated goal that is different from the stated goal of the group.)

V. Implementing the Solution

    A. Be sure that decisions on implementation are also arrived at through consensus.

    B. Be sure someone accurately summarizes the decision and puts it in writing.

VI. Evaluating the Solution

    A. Everyone should also agree on the method to be used in evaluating the solution.

    B. Agree that the solution is open for revision, but only through the group's participation, and not unilaterally.

    C. Agree on a future date for evaluating the success (or failure) of the solution.

Consensus Decision Making

Consensus is the end product of a decision making, problem solving process involving a group of persons who understand their assigned task and are highly motivated to complete it. Success will depend largely on how willing each person in the group is to commit his time and energy to a solution. Consensus problem solving requires making full use of available resources; this means that each member of the group must feel responsible for involving every other member of the group in the discussion. It must be understood, furthermore, that every decision must be a group decision acceptable to every member of the group on rational grounds, even though it may not be any particular member's first choice. **In other words, complete unanimity is not the goal of consensus -- it is rarely achieved.** In place of unanimous decisions, consensus strives for group decisions where everyone involved feels reasonably satisfied with the outcome. When all group members feel this way, the group has reached consensus, and the judgment may be entered as a group decision.

Willingness to listen and an overriding concern for the success of the group effort are the two attitudes necessary for true consensus. <u>Try to work within the following guidelines</u>:

A. Avoid arguing excessively for your own choices. Present your opinions as clearly and as logically as you can, but then listen attentively to other persons' reactions and to their opinions.

B. Try constantly to avoid allowing anyone in the group to feel he or she has "lost" and that someone else has "won." The need to win -- to employ verbal power to manipulate others -- on the part of any member of the group will seriously damage the effectiveness of the group's work. Look, instead, for the "next-most-acceptable" alternative, so that everyone will feel he or she has been acknowledged and has contributed.

C. Do not change your mind simply to avoid conflict and to reach agreement quickly. This point becomes increasingly important the longer the group works on its task. The passage of time is itself the worst enemy of consensus. Although people differ in this respect, almost everyone will eventually reach their limit of tolerance for any discussion and become impatient or bored with the problem-solving task. If you do change your mind, provide a reason why you changed your mind.

D. Avoid conflict-reducing techniques such as majority vote, averaging of individual choices, and bargaining. The "I'll-give-you-this-if-you-give-me-that" approach to problem solving violates in fundamental ways the spirit of consensus. In any important relationship, we don't give in order to get; we give, and we receive, unconditionally. The same should be true of consensus.

E. Remember that differences of opinion are natural and are to be encouraged. Seek them out, and involve everyone in the decision process. Disagreement generates a wider range of information and opinion, which in turn contributes to better solutions.

Roles Group Members Assume

As you approach working with a small group of people, it is important to understand that the outcome of the group can be affected by how each member participates in the group process. In general we can think of group members as having the potential to assume three types of roles within the group. One type of role that is played by group members is the role that attends to the "task" of the group. The second type of role is one that attends to the "feelings" and "confirmation" of members of the group. The third type of role is one that holds the group together in a "cohesive" manner. Cohesiveness is related to the concept of synergy in that the cohesive group will be experiencing high synergy while the group which lacks cohesiveness will be experiencing low synergy. The obvious conclusion is that as members of a group we want to take on the roles that will accomplish the task, validate each member of the group, and foster high cohesiveness.

Roles Group Members Should Play

INITIATE A TOPIC OR BEGIN THE DISCUSSION: This group member begins the discussion during a particular meeting, shifts the discussion to a new topic, suggests a different answer to some problem being considered, or changes the focus of the discussion for a reason.

ASK QUESTIONS: Questions may be seeking further information, clarifying some point being made in the discussion, or soliciting an opinion from another group member.

GIVE OPINIONS: All group members should give their opinions about topics in a group discussion.

SHARE OR ELABORATE ON INFORMATION: Group members who know information about topics for discussion should share the information or should "piggyback" on other members' discussion by elaborating on that information.

ACT AS LEADER: Sometimes it is evident that someone in the group needs to guide the discussion of the group. Any member of the group can take on a leadership role when needed.

ACT AS RECORDER: A group member should volunteer for this role if a record of the discussion is needed for some reason.

EVALUATE A POINT OF VIEW: This is an analytical role in which a group member will state his or her evaluation of some point in the discussion.

DEFINE THE PROCEDURES OF THE GROUP: Often the group member who takes on this role will use "metadiscussion" or "discussion about the discussion" to describe the procedures of the group. The group member assuming this role may desire to keep the group working productively or to show the group how well (or poorly) they may have been working.

SUMMARIZE: All members of the group should summarize the statements of other group members, and, when appropriate, summarize the total discussion to the current point.

VERIFY/CLARIFY INFORMATION OR OPINION: A group member will check information or opinion with the group member who gave the information or opinion.

GATEKEEPER/EXPEDITER: Will encourage less talkative members to participate or will seek ways to limit lengthy statements of others.

Roles Group Members Should Avoid

AGGRESSOR, BLOCKER, DOMINATOR, or ALWAYS NEGATIVE: Destroys status of other group members, is generally negative or disagreeable, makes an effort to take over the entire group.

ASSIGNMENT: Seminar

Unlike a "speech" or "presentation," the seminar is an *impromptu* activity. In other words, you don't know ahead of time what you're going to say, because you don't know what statements others will make, what questions they will raise, or what new knowledge will be created as the discussion progresses. All you know before hand is the particular subject your group has been assigned to discuss. You know what the *subject* of the discussion is, but not what you will say about it.

A suggested structure of this activity:

1. Have a *maximum* of 15 participants. Any more than 15 make the impromptu character of the discussion impossible.

2. If the seminar is going to be recorded, arrange the chairs in a tight semicircle, with the camera at the open end. Otherwise, form the group into a circle. (Be sure there are no empty chairs, since they, in a mysterious way, become an "energy drain.")

3. The seminar is a true collaborative learning activity. Once the discussion begins, the students are **completely** on their own, practicing the group communication skills as well as they can. There may be an awkward period of hesitation and silence at first, until the necessary "risk-taking" begins.

4. The *seminar* discussion topic may be a speech, a short story, a case study, a problem of concern, just so long as there is some time for preparation before the discussion.

5. The *seminar* discussion takes place during one class hour. In the following hour, explore the dynamics of the seminar. How do the participants feel about the experience? What worked; what didn't work? If the seminar is videotaped, a useful activity for the next meeting is to play back some of the tape to see how well participants are using the four skills. At some point, the instructor should stop the tape so you can discuss the following questions in groups of 3 or 4.

   a) What were we doing well and should continue doing in future discussions?

   b) What were some things that we could have done better, and what would each group member do differently in future discussions?

How do students prepare for the seminar?

Since this is an *impromptu* activity, there are only a few things to do, but these must be done very conscientiously if you are to contribute to the success of the discussion:

1. Study the assigned speech manuscript or video, short story, case study, or problem. *Highlight* key passages. Write brief *comments or questions* in the margin. Be **active, assertive** as a reader, ready to contribute to the discussion. Don't feel you have to come with the story or problem "all figured out." That will happen in the discussion. It's enough to have some good questions for the group; don't worry yet about *answers*.

2. To help the discussion get started, you might prepare one or two good "open-ended" questions. By "open-ended" we mean questions for which there is room for opinions and discussion. The purpose of such questions is to help get things going in a useful, potentially fruitful, direction. Avoid "dead-end" questions at one extreme: e.g., "How many brothers and sisters did Sarty

have?" This is a factual question that, once answered, has no place to go. Or, at the other extreme, avoid questions which are so general, so "large," that they can only be answered at the *end* of the discussion; e.g., "Does anyone have any idea what the story means?" or, "What were some significant symbols?"

3. Review the four skills needed for successful participation in a group discussion. (see page 80) Come to the discussion well aware of what you need to do to help the group be successful.

Response Form: **Seminar Discussion**

Name_____

1. What was the speech, story, case study or problem your seminar group addressed?

2. Describe some of the assertive behaviors you observed during the discussion.

3. What would you say about your own participation in the discussion?

4. What would you say about the progress of the group during the discussion?

Critique Form: **Seminar Discussion**

Hand this page to the Instructor when requested.

SEMINAR PARTICIPATION   **(25 pts)**   **NAME**_____

1.   REFLECTIVE LISTENING (Actively Listening to Others)

2.   CLEAR SENDING (Expressing ideas clearly and concretely)

3.   ENCOURAGING PARTICIPATION OF ALL MEMBERS

4.   HELPING MOVE THE GROUP TO A CONCLUSION

ROLES RELATED TO CLEAR SENDING	ROLES RELATED TO REFLECTIVE LISTENING
_____Initiate Topic, Begin Discussion	_____Summarize
_____Ask Questions	_____Verify Information
_____Give Opinions	_____Verify Opinion
_____Share/Elaborate on Information	_____Clarify Information
_____Act as Leader	_____Clarify Opinion
_____Act as Recorder	_____Other (explain)
_____Evaluate a Point of View	
_____Define the Procedures	
_____Other (explain)	

ASSIGNMENT: Problem Solving Discussion

A Panel Discussion is presented for the purpose of informing the audience about a topic of some relevance. For purposes of this assignment, members of your small group will participate in a problem solving or decision making experience that will be videotaped. Group members will then watch the videotape to analyze the communication and discussion behaviors of the group. It will be this analysis that will be presented in the form of a Panel Discussion during a later class period.

DAY 1: Group members select a case study or problem scenario from those provided by the instructor. You may discuss the process by which you will attempt to solve the problem, but do not discuss the problem itself. Privately, after class, you may do any research you wish in order to prepare for the discussion.

DAY 2: Group members discuss the case study or problem while being videotaped for approximately 30 minutes. Delivery style should be Impromptu. You should follow the guidelines for successful group discussion that include Reflective Listening, Clear Sending, and playing the appropriate roles to facilitate the discussion when necessary. You should follow the Problem Solving Method on page 88. It is not necessary to reach a consensus decision about the solution to your problem, but at all times during the discussion, it should be obvious that the group is attempting to solve the problem.

DAY 3: Group members meet to view the videotape of their discussion. During the first viewing of the video tape group members will want to take note generally of how the group followed the guidelines for successful discussion, which members played which types of roles during the discussion, and how well the group followed the guidelines for problem solving. In other words, you will be looking for the communication behaviors that were exhibited by group members during a problem solving discussion.

Before the second viewing of the videotape, group members need to assign the following sub-topics. Each group member will be responsible for the analysis of one of the sub-topics. (In some cases, two group members may work together to analyze one sub-topic.)

SUB-TOPICS FOR ANALYSIS

1. Listening behaviors within the group with particular attention to Reflective Listening.
2. Clear and Congruent Sending behaviors within the group with particular attention to sending concrete messages.
3. The roles group members assumed during the discussion.
4. How the group managed the problem solving process with particular attention to how the group progressed through the problem solving steps.
5. The synergy within the group and how the synergy changed during the time of the discussion.
6. Consensus decision making.
7. Passive, Assertive, Aggressive Behaviors.
8. Risks taken during discussion.
9. Flight Behaviors used or avoided during the discussion.
10. The value/usefulness of the case study selected by the group in being able to complete the assignment.
11. Use of the four skills for successful group participation.
12. The group may decide that there is some topic that is unique to their particular group discussion which one member may wish to analyze. If this is the case, the group should propose this unique topic to the instructor for approval.

DAY 4: Group members share their analyses and plan their presentation for the class.

SPECIFICS FOR GROUP PRESENTATION: Analysis of a Problem Solving Discussion

1. Each group will have 30 minutes to present the results of their analyses.

2. The Form of the Group Presentation includes the following:

   INTRODUCTION
   - Describe the specifics of the problem the group discussed.
   - Introduce the speakers and speaking order to the audience.

   SPEECHES OF ANALYSIS
   - Each group member presents his or her analysis of the sub-topic.
   - Each group member writes his or her speech outline using the outlining instructions on page 145. (For examples see page 103.) Staple page 101 to the front of the outline.
   - Each speech is approximately 4 minutes long.
   - Each speech should contain:
     a) at least two "points" of analysis.
     b) concrete examples from the tape that illustrate the points of analysis.
     c) your conclusion about the relative success of the group in terms of the particular sub-topic.
     d) a speech delivery that is extemporaneous in style supported with eye contact, clear sending and gestures.

   CONCLUSION
   - Video Clip: Members of the group should select a 30 to 60 second "clip" to show the audience. Set up the "clip" with your rationale for why you selected this particular section of the tape to show the audience.
   - Answer any questions from the audience.

NOTE: A possible source for the case studies for this assignment is:

Berko, R. M., Wolvin, A. D. and Wolvin, D. R. 1989. Communicating: A Social and Career Focus. Fourth Ed. Boston, MA: Houghton Mifflin Co.

The exercise asks students to make jury type decisions for a number of different cases.

Response Form: **Problem Solving Discussion**

NAME_____

1. List the number of your group and the case study your group analyzed.

2. Discuss the success of your group in terms of:
   a. Analyzing the case

   b. Assisting each other in preparation

   c. Presenting your analysis to the class

3. If your presentation was videotaped:
   a. Does the videotape show you more or less comfortable and confident than you really were?

   b. What about your delivery pleases you, and what will you change before your next speech?

PEER FEEDBACK

NAME OF GROUP MEMBER   POINTS AWARDED

1.

2.

3.

4.

5.

6.

7.

8.

Critique Form: **Problem Solving Discussion**

<u>Include with Outline</u>

NAME_____

The evaluation will be based on how well you meet the requirements.

INDIVIDUAL OUTLINE   15 points

INDIVIDUAL SPEECH AS DELIVERED   30 points
    Speech Organization
    Thesis
    Preview of Main Points

    Speech Content
        Two Main Points clearly stated
        Development of ideas and examples

    Speech Delivery   Extemporaneous
        Loud, clear voice
        Eye contact
        Gestures

OVERALL GROUP PRESENTATION   20 points
    Introduction to Group Presentation
    Clear Planning
    Logical Progression of Sub-Topics
    Transitions used between Parts
    Pattern of Organization obvious
    Introductions/Conclusions included
    Group Conclusion to the Presentation
    Lack of Distractions from group members during presentation

GROUP PARTICIPATION   10 points

    Daily preparation

    Daily attendance

    Daily contributions

PEER EVALUATION   10 points

    Value of contributions

    Commitment to group effort

Examples: **Sample Outlines for Speeches**

Outline for Sub-Topic: Four Group Skills

By Dawn Harrington
(Reprinted with permission.)

INTRODUCTION

Have you ever been in a discussion with a large group? Well, if you come from a fairly large family like I do, then you have. Have you ever had to reach a consensus with that large group? Well, my family does sometimes have difficulty reaching consensus when we are trying to make a decision, but my family hasn't yet been introduced to the skills for group discussion that we are learning in this course. There are four useful skills for trying to reach a consensus which include the following: Listening to others, Expressing ideas clearly and concretely, Encouraging participation of all members, and Helping move the group to a conclusion. Luckily, my class group knew about these skills before even attempting to come to a consensus.

THESIS

Today, I will be elaborating on those skills to show how at times we used the four skills effectively and at other times, when we didn't seem to be using the skills enough.

BODY

I. Our group used the four skills (Listening to others, Expressing ideas clearly and concretely, Encouraging Participation of all members, and, Helping move the group to a conclusion) very effectively at times.

    A. At the beginning the group used the first two skills very effectively.

        1. We started off by listening to each others perception of the problem.

            a. Kristine read the problem out loud first.

            b. Everyone listened so effectively, that it led to people being able to talk about their personal bouts with this problem.

        2. Everyone had their chance when they felt that they could express their ideas clearly and concretely.

            a. Fernando expressed that to tell the parents wouldn't be such a good idea.

            b. Inbal suggested that the girl should introduce the boy as a friend first.

    B. Towards the middle and the end of the discussion is when the group started to use skills three and four effectively.

        1. When we got more comfortable with each other is when we started to encourage participation of all the members.

      a. Fernando encouraged Inbal by telling her that she had a great idea.

      b. Monica told Inbal that her idea was a good one also.

   2. When the group felt good about the decisions that it was making, it started to naturally move towards a conclusion.

      a. When we all agreed on the solution that the girl should tell her parents we affirmed each others decision.

      b. Everyone in the group started to nod their heads a lot and to get a little excited about reaching an agreement.

II. At times our group didn't use two of the skills and our communication suffered because of it.

  A. When our group didn't listen to one another or didn't send their ideas clearly and concretely our communication suffered.

   1. When a group member came late and hadn't been able to listen to what had gone on in the group previously, our discussion had to slow down for them to catch up.

   2. Once, when someone didn't articulate loud enough and had to repeat themselves it slowed the group down a bit.

  B. When a person became passive and didn't offer any solutions it slowed down the group's discussion process.

   1. For a long time Jason remained passive and just listened to everyone else's opinions.

   2. People stopped listening to each other and just started making random statements thinking that they were getting their opinions heard.

CONCLUSION

    In the end, we were able to come to a consensus because we used the four skills effectively. Sure, there were times that we fell off track but there was always someone in the group who put us back on track and back to using the four skills again. When it comes to effective consensus making, these four skills are definitely needed: Listening to others, Expressing ideas clearly and concretely, Encouraging participation of all members, and lastly, Helping move the group to a conclusion. In our group, we learned a lot about how to effectively participate in a group discussion by watching the video and talking about how effective we were in using these skills.

Outline for Sub-topic: Consensus Decision Making

By Lynette Fruen
(Reprinted with permission)

INTRODUCTION

Have you ever been in a meeting where someone makes the decision for you? How did you feel?
Have you ever had someone not listen to you? How did you feel? Have you ever had to make many
decisions that involved others in order to reach a common goal?

THESIS

Today I will describe how Consensus Decision Making worked within our group by first talking
about how our group did or did not present opinions clearly and listen attentively, and second, how our
group did or did not use conflict-reducing techniques.

BODY

I.   First I will talk about how our group had varying rates of success in presenting opinions clearly and
      listening attentively.

      A. During our first major difference of opinion, we listened attentively and were able to express our
          opinions clearly enough in order to reach a consensus.

          1. Anthony first stated that he selected the First Aid Kit as the fourth item and most members
              agreed with the placement.

          2. Renee then stated that she selected the Constellation Map, to which Mike also agreed.

          3. Anthony expressed his concern about providing care for the injured crewmembers while Renee
              expressed concerns that the kit only contained injection needles.

          4. After Neil, Mike, and Anthony clarified points; I discussed how the needles could be used to
              inject water into the food packets in order to eat.

          5. Renee, Mike and the rest of the group all agreed that the fourth item should be the first aid Kit,
              by either saying so or nodding, and it was recorded.

      B. As the group encountered greater differences of opinion on priority, presenting our opinions and
          listening attentively became more difficult and our consensus decision-making suffered.

          1. Multiple people were trying to talk at the same time making it difficult to hear peoples'
              opinions.

          2. Group members were interrupted while asking questions or voicing their opinions, while others
              sat silently not voicing any opinion for or against a particular item.

3. Due to the variety of priorities and opinions, clarification was needed as to the priority number we were working on and what had been decided.

4. We did listen attentively as Anthony recapped what he thought had been decided on only to find out that the perceived order was incorrect.

II. Second, I will talk about how effective our group was at using or not using conflict-reducing techniques.

   A. Most group members did not avoid conflict in order to reach an agreement quickly.

      1. Renee and Anthony often disagreed on the importance and use of items, such as the map, heater, and signal flares.

      2. Other members either expanded on comments that were made, asked questions, provided factual information, or stated their placement of the item.

      3. When Renee decided to change her mind to accept the life raft instead of her original choice, she gave a reason why she was changing her mind stating, "The life raft was probably more resourceful."

   B. Our group had one instance of using conflict-reducing techniques.

      1. After a lengthy discussion on whether the constellation map or the portable heater should be selected as the fifth priority, two members of our group bargained for placement.

         a. Kevin asked, "If #5 is the map, would #6 be the portable heater?"
         b. Renee responded, "Yes."
         c. Kevin then replied, "I'm willing to agree with that as long as the portable heating unit follows that."

      2. As a result of the bargain, other group members didn't comment on what they had for the 6th spot therefore, their choices were never considered against the value of the heater.

CONCLUSION

Although our group was able to prioritize 10 items, and generally did not avoid conflicts to reach agreements quickly, according to Communication Skills for Collaborative Learning by Luotto and Stoll, one of the attitudes that is needed for true consensus in the willingness to listen. Our group struggled with listening for the majority of our problem solving process, with the exception of our first disagreement, where we listened much more attentively which enabled us to present our opinions more clearly in order to reach a group consensus.

ASSIGNMENT: Symposium using a Single Class Topic

Requirements

1. Your group will decide on a topic related to the class theme. Be Creative (Ideas for class themes: Pluralism, Democracy, Upcoming Elections)

2. Members of the group will research the focus you have agreed upon. Each group member should find a minimum of three outside sources of information. Share your research with everyone else.

3. Your task is to present a 45-minute symposium (includes individual speeches by each member) in which you add to our understanding of the class topic. Class time will be provided to define sub-topics, organize presentation, help each other edit outlines, write transitions, etc. Practice assertive communication skills in your group discussions. Take risks.

4. Presentation should be engaging and make use of a variety of support forms.

5. An introduction and conclusion should be clearly identifiable. All group members are graded on the effectiveness of the introduction and conclusion. These are to be typed out and handed in with individual outlines on the day of your presentation. The group introduction must include a group thesis statement that makes clear the connection between your specific focus and the class theme.

6. Coherent transitions should bridge each main point of your presentation.

7. Individual outlines (instructions on page 145) are due the day of your speech in the order of presenters. Please staple page 109 to the front of your individual outline.

8. Each individual speech should contain a clear Thesis statement, contain at least two main points, make use of adequate supporting information, be delivered in extemporaneous style, and make use of audio, visual aides as appropriate.

9. The group is responsible for bringing an 8mm videotape on the day of your presentation.

10. You are required to view the tape of your presentation, assess your skills as a speaker, and make necessary improvements prior to the next speaking round.

Class Theme_____

Our Specific Group Focus_____

Symposium Presentation Due_____

Critique Form: **Symposium Discussion**

<u>Include with Outline</u>

NAME_____

The evaluation will be based on how well you meet the requirements.

INDIVIDUAL OUTLINE   15 points

INDIVIDUAL SPEECH AS DELIVERED   30 points
     Speech Organization
     Thesis
     Preview of Main Points

     Speech Content
          Two Main Points clearly stated
          Development of ideas and examples

     Speech Delivery   Extemporaneous
          Loud, clear voice
          Eye contact
          Gestures

OVERALL GROUP PRESENTATION   20 points
     Introduction to Group Presentation
     Clear Planning
     Logical Progression of Sub-Topics
     Transitions used between Parts
     Pattern of Organization obvious
     Introductions/Conclusions included
     Group Conclusion to the Presentation
     Lack of Distractions from group members during presentation

GROUP PARTICIPATION   10 points

     Daily preparation

     Daily attendance

     Daily contributions

PEER EVALUATION   10 points

     Value of contributions

     Commitment to group effort

ASSIGNMENT: Symposium Using a Current Problem or Issue

The definition of this form of a Symposium Discussion is a presentation by a panel of student experts. Panel members will first give a series of speeches, which explain their point of view and then answer questions from the audience members. This assignment asks your group to research and solve a problem, which is of current interest to all of the members of the class.

REQUIREMENTS OF THE ASSIGNMENT

1. The group will select a topic from the list provided in class.

2. Members of the group will research the topic in order to define the parameters of the discussion. The depth of research should result in each member of the group finding at least three sources of information, which s/he can use during the speech.

3. During class time, students will meet with their groups. Follow the Problem Solving Method (see page 88), using all steps, which relate to your particular topic.

4. The topic should be sub-divided to include at least all of the following:
    a) The nature and scope of the problem
    b) The history of the problem
    c) The relative seriousness of the problem as the group sees it
    d) The criteria the group has devised for solving the problem
    e) The possible solutions to the problem
    f) The advantages and disadvantages to the solutions
    g) The solution the group proposes and the relative merits of that solution

5. The group symposium (including speeches by each member of the group) should be 45 minutes long.

6. An Introduction and Conclusion should be clearly identifiable in the symposium presentation.

7. Smooth and logical transitions should be used between the Introduction and the first speech, between all subsequent speeches, and between the last speech and the Conclusion.

8. Each speech should contain a clear Thesis Statement and Preview of Main Points.

9. Individual speeches will be delivered in an extemporaneous style.

10. A typed full sentence outline will be submitted by each member of the group on the day of the symposium presentation. (For examples see page 103; for outlining instructions see page 145)

As you can see, this is a progressive symposium -- meaning that each speech depends on the speeches before it in order to make "sense" to the audience. In that way, this activity is **truly collaborative** in that all members of the group need to be able to depend on each other to successfully present their part of the symposium.

ASSIGNMENT: Collaborating to Study Controversial Issues

This activity was prepared by Sally Wood, a De Anza College Reading Instructor for students in a combined Reading and Writing class she teaches with Writing Instructor Jean Miller. (Reprinted with permission.)

INTRODUCTION

The goals for this activity are to:
- research, read and thoroughly analyze three long articles on their issue;
- collaborate with their classmates assigned the same issue to plan and deliver an oral presentation which covers both the pro and con arguments of the issue, and
- write an individual essay in which the student not only explains both the pro and con arguments of the issue but also states and supports which side s/he favors.

PROCEDURE OF IMPLEMENTING THE PROJECT

The first stage of the project takes approximately two weeks. During this period, students find and read news articles on current controversial issues. They typically find material on topics such as euthanasia, legalizing drugs, abortion, and gays in the military. At the end of this reading period, they participate in a brainstorming activity during which they state issues they would like to study further. The instructor writes the suggested issues on the chalkboard, and the class discusses each, considering whether there are definite pro and con arguments involved and if reading materials would be readily available to give enough information on the issue. Next, by a show of hands, students indicate which issues they like best, and the most popular are selected.

Students give the instructor a note on which they prioritize the three issues that interest them the most, and are placed in groups of three to five based primarily on their choices.

The second stage of the project is to find information on the issues. The library staff gives an orientation to the facilities and assists the groups in finding articles of appropriate difficulty level and length. Though individuals are encouraged to find some articles on their own, they are allowed also to share one or two with group members. They know that within the group they need to find readings that cover both the pro and con arguments on the issue.

Next, individuals read and do a written analysis of each of three lengthy articles, which they turn in to the instructor. The analysis includes identifying the author's thesis, tones, purpose, approach (subjective or objective), and use of denotative and/or connotative language. In the final section of their analysis, they must write two to four paragraphs in which they state and explain why they are for or against the issue.

During the third stage of the project, the students meet in their groups both in and out of class to plan their fifteen to twenty minute oral presentation. They are encouraged to try to develop a creative presentation which will interest their audience. Some formats which students have used that were well received are listed below in **"Ideas for Group Presentations."** Students are reminded to make clear in their presentation, both the pro and con arguments of the issue and to be sure all group members participate in some way. When groups have finished planning their presentation, they complete and submit the **Group Presentation Worksheet** (see page 115). After each group gives its presentation, the audience evaluates and writes feedback comments using the **Evaluation Form** (see page 117).

For the final stage of the project, students are given a week to draft, discuss with group members, edit, and then write an essay about their issue. In this essay they are required to explain both the pro and con arguments of the issue and state which side they favor. They must support their opinion with clear, concrete examples from their research or from personal experience.

This project allows students to demonstrate and reinforce many reading, critical thinking, and writing strategies they have been working on for the term. They enjoy the presentations and often become quite involved in asking questions and arguing their own views. Though the project, in the above form, takes two to three weeks, it can be streamlined in the following ways:

- Instead of conducting an orientation and finding materials in the library, the instructor can assign articles from the anthology being used for the course or from news publications;

- Requiring students to write an essay could be eliminated if the project is being used in a class that does not demand such writing.

REMINDER
If one is to use this project as a whole, it is important to give students very specific instructions. First, present an overview of the assignment and explain the objectives, and then provide individuals with specific directions for each stage of the project. It is especially helpful to explain the type and length of articles students should find because short articles often lack substantial pro and/or con arguments.

Ideas for Group Presentations

Your group may use one of the following formats or create one of its own. Remember that having your audience participate makes the presentation more interesting to them and easier for you. You may want to use video or audio equipment, illustrations, handouts, or costumes. Also, consider allowing time after your presentation for the audience to ask questions and engage in some discussion.

1. Compare and/or contrast two people who have been involved in an incident concerning the issue.

2. Broadcast a radio or TV editorial and a response stating both sides of the issue (use sound effects or background music if you wish).

3. Debate both sides of the issue.

4. Dramatize an incident concerning the issue.

5. Hold a mock trial with defendant, plaintiff, and/or witnesses presenting various arguments on the issue.

6. Conduct an opinion poll of the class members and/or people outside of the class; relate their responses to arguments for both sides of the issue.

7. Make and explain an illustration about the issue.

8. Introduce your presentation by giving the class a quiz about the issue or ask them to state which side of the issue they favor.

Worksheet: Group Presentation

Group_____

ISSUE:

1.   Please provide a detailed explanation of the format of your group's presentation.

2.   Please explain the role and contribution of each team member:

    a.   Name:_____

            Contribution:

    b.   Name:_____

            Contribution:

    c.   Name:_____

            Contribution:

    d.   Name:_____

            Contribution:

    e.   Name:_____

            Contribution:

3.   What handouts, if any, do you plan to use?

4.   Will you need any of the following equipment?

        ___TV monitor   ___VCR   ___tape player

        ___any other (please explain):

Evaluation Form: **Controversial Issue Presentation**

*Group Issue:*_____

Criteria: 1 = inadequate; 2 = poor; 3 = average; 4 = good; 5 = excellent
1. Group presented both pro and con arguments
    (including statistics, examples and quotes)   1 2 3 4 5
2. A balance of pro and con arguments was presented   1 2 3 4 5
3. Arguments presented were valid   1 2 3 4 5
4. All members participated equally   1 2 3 4 5
5. Creativity of presentation   1 2 3 4 5
6. Thoroughness of presentation   1 2 3 4 5
7. Audience participation: 1 2 3 4 5
8. Overall Group Score: 1 2 3 4 5
COMMENTS FOR THE GROUP:

Evaluation Form: **Controversial Issue Presentation**

*Group Issue:*_____

Criteria: 1 = inadequate; 2 = poor; 3 = average; 4 = good; 5 = excellent
1. Group presented both pro and con arguments
    (including statistics, examples and quotes)   1 2 3 4 5
2. A balance of pro and con arguments was presented   1 2 3 4 5
3. Arguments presented were valid   1 2 3 4 5
4. All members participated equally   1 2 3 4 5
5. Creativity of presentation   1 2 3 4 5
6. Thoroughness of presentation   1 2 3 4 5
7. Audience participation: 1 2 3 4 5
8. Overall Group Score: 1 2 3 4 5
COMMENTS FOR THE GROUP:

Evaluation Form: **Controversial Issue Presentation**

*Group Issue:*_____

Criteria: 1 = inadequate; 2 = poor; 3 = average; 4 = good; 5 = excellent
1. Group presented both pro and con arguments
    (including statistics, examples and quotes)   1 2 3 4 5
2. A balance of pro and con arguments was presented   1 2 3 4 5
3. Arguments presented were valid   1 2 3 4 5
4. All members participated equally   1 2 3 4 5
5. Creativity of presentation   1 2 3 4 5
6. Thoroughness of presentation   1 2 3 4 5
7. Audience participation: 1 2 3 4 5
8. Overall Group Score: 1 2 3 4 5
COMMENTS FOR THE GROUP:

Evaluation Form: **Controversial Issue Presentation**

*Group Issue:*_____

Criteria: 1 = inadequate; 2 = poor; 3 = average; 4 = good; 5 = excellent
1. Group presented both pro and con arguments
    (including statistics, examples and quotes)   1 2 3 4 5
2. A balance of pro and con arguments was presented   1 2 3 4 5
3. Arguments presented were valid   1 2 3 4 5
4. All members participated equally   1 2 3 4 5
5. Creativity of presentation   1 2 3 4 5
6. Thoroughness of presentation   1 2 3 4 5
7. Audience participation: 1 2 3 4 5
8. Overall Group Score: 1 2 3 4 5
COMMENTS FOR THE GROUP:

Evaluation Form: **Controversial Issue Presentation**

*Group Issue:*_____

Criteria: 1 = inadequate; 2 = poor; 3 = average; 4 = good; 5 = excellent
1. Group presented both pro and con arguments
    (including statistics, examples and quotes)   1 2 3 4 5
2. A balance of pro and con arguments was presented   1 2 3 4 5
3. Arguments presented were valid   1 2 3 4 5
4. All members participated equally   1 2 3 4 5
5. Creativity of presentation   1 2 3 4 5
6. Thoroughness of presentation   1 2 3 4 5
7. Audience participation: 1 2 3 4 5
8. Overall Group Score: 1 2 3 4 5
COMMENTS FOR THE GROUP:

Evaluation Form: **Controversial Issue Presentation**

*Group Issue:*_____

Criteria: 1 = inadequate; 2 = poor; 3 = average; 4 = good; 5 = excellent
1. Group presented both pro and con arguments
    (including statistics, examples and quotes)   1 2 3 4 5
2. A balance of pro and con arguments was presented   1 2 3 4 5
3. Arguments presented were valid   1 2 3 4 5
4. All members participated equally   1 2 3 4 5
5. Creativity of presentation   1 2 3 4 5
6. Thoroughness of presentation   1 2 3 4 5
7. Audience participation: 1 2 3 4 5
8. Overall Group Score: 1 2 3 4 5
COMMENTS FOR THE GROUP:

Group Investigation in the University Classroom

By Shlomo Sharan, School of Education, Tel-Aviv University, Israel. (Reprinted with permission.)
This example is a shortened version of the Group Investigation Technique. The complete version is in:
Sharan, Y. and Sharan, S. 1992. Expanding Cooperative Learning Through Group Investigation. New
York, NY: Teachers College, Columbia University.

The Group Investigation approach seeks to stimulate learning as an "inside to outside" process
rather than an "outside to inside" process, as is commonly practiced even in most Cooperative Learning
methods. That is to say, Group Investigation organizes students to seek and solve problems in given areas
of study, and to understand, and try to solve these problems. Group Investigation also can be used to
produce knowledge through use and synthesis of a wide variety of informational sources and experiences.
This approach stands in contrast with those methods where students are expected to learn (often used
synonymously with memorize) or consume quantities of knowledge predetermined by the teacher. In this
sense, Group Investigation was designed to follow the steps typical of mature research: to test hypotheses
formulated in advance by those who seek to acquire the information necessary to determine whether the
hypotheses support the theory from which they were derived. Group Investigation is thus an exercise in the
pursuit of knowledge, and not in the consumption of given knowledge. However, this pursuit of knowledge
is conducted with a small number of peers who interact with one another in many ways during their
collective effort to study and solve a problem.

GROUP INVESTIGATION AND THE FOUR I'S

Group Investigation works effectively because it incorporates four features which are consistent
with good practice in teaching and learning: Investigation, Interaction, Interpretation and Intrinsic
Motivation.

Investigation. This feature is Group Investigation's distinguishing characteristic, and the entire
class must be directed toward this form of learning in order to create the social environment that sustains
this approach. Small groups of students, rarely numbering more than five per group and usually only four,
engage in planning precisely what the group wishes to investigate as part of the class' broad topic. The
group also plans how and where it will seek information or experiences relevant to the topic they choose. It
is suggested that the topic be formulated as a problem that requires solution. (Why do human beings walk
on two feet? What cultural influence did China receive from India? What are the basic features of prophecy
in ancient Israel versus philosophy in ancient Greece? What kinds of effects does demographic change in
Africa, India and China have on ecological problems in those countries? What are the major moral,
philosophical and practical implications of Galileo's discovery that the earth revolves around the sun?)

One way of generating a series of problems that relate to a central class wide topic is to have the
class proceed through a series of steps whereby it proposes and lists problems. These problems can then be
organized into categories and selected by the different groups in the class as their topics for investigation.
For example, pairs of students can be asked to write down all the problems they consider a necessary part of
understanding a broad topic introduced by the instructor. Pairs sitting close to one another are then
combined into fours, and two fours can be combined later into groups of eight. Each stage lasts only a few
minutes, although the last stage of octets requires more time. At each stage, the component groups (of two,
four or eight members) generate lists of suggestions for sub-topics needing study, compare their lists,
eliminate duplication and continue to suggest new problems or sub-topics that need study to achieve a broad
understanding of the major topic at hand. At the level of the octets, students in each group are asked to
categorize all of the suggestions listed thus far into a small number of categories. All of these categories
from each octet in the class are posted on a placard or on a blackboard, duplications eliminated, and a series

of topics are identified as appropriate for investigation. This latter step is carried out with the entire class as a whole.

Students are counseled about locating sources of information needed for various investigations, such as printed materials in libraries, sites to be visited, people to be interviewed, experiments to be conducted, and observations to be made. The variety and richness of the materials depend, of course, upon local conditions and upon the initiative of the instructor and the students.

Interaction. During the process of carrying out these stages, the students, working in small groups, will interact with one another in many different ways including exchanging ideas, feelings, and points of view, mutual assisting, and assuming responsibility for different aspects of the work to be done. Of course, investigations can always be performed by individuals, and in some of the humanities (history, literature, etc.) the tradition of individual research is still very strong. However, given the complexity of the information needed, research in many fields by persons working entirely alone is becoming less common, particularly in the natural and social sciences. The point is not so much that investigation **can** be done by individuals, but that it can also be accomplished in a very rewarding and motivating way by small groups of individuals, working together. This small-group setting for investigation provides many positive features that cannot be experienced by individuals working alone, namely, the entire dimension of constant communication with others about a topic of common concern.

Interpretation. Information is made meaningful when it is placed in a broader context by connecting to existing ideas and relating to past experiences. Knowledge emerges when information is made meaningful; it is not inherent in the information itself. The small group setting is an ideal forum for having students attribute meaning to the information they uncover about the problem at hand, and hence to have that information gradually become knowledge for those students. Such knowledge is all the more important to students because they interpreted its meaning rather than had the meaning presented by the instructor as interpreted by him/herself or other scholars. Interpretation is thus an essential feature in the pursuit of knowledge and can be greatly enhanced by the communication occurring between members of small groups.

Intrinsic Motivation. Research and theory in teaching and learning suggest that the combined functioning of the three I's just described will activate and sustain students' genuine interest in the subject they study. Thus, students will devote themselves to their investigation not only because they want a good grade, but also because the topic engages their interest. The study of academic subject matter out of interest rather than for external reward is an essential element in all quality education. Failure to engage students' genuine interest in the pursuit of knowledge is a widespread and deeply regrettable feature of today's education at all levels. Granted; not all learning experiences can or need be intrinsically motivated, it is still of significant importance that some critical mass of students' educational experiences be so motivated if they are to cultivate any interest in learning that will survive their years in formal educational settings. Group Investigation invites students to take an active role in determining the content and method of study they pursue within an interactive social context. Expanding students' control over their learning behavior, together with the motivating aspects of a relatively free form of peer interaction devoted to a common goal, all appear to promote and heighten students' intrinsic interest in the work of investigating a topic. Hence, intrinsic motivation is one anticipated result of implementing the first three of the four I's.

When all four I's operate as anticipated, Group Investigation typically leads to many other beneficial results including increases in academic achievement, and improved relations between students of different social classes and ethnic groups (Sharan & Sharan, 1992).

THE SIX STAGES OF GROUP INVESTIGATION

The four I's are embodied in the procedures to be carried out by students when conducting a study according to the Group Investigation method. These procedures can be divided into six consecutive stages.

Stage 1: Class Determines Subtopics and Organizes Into Research Groups. Students scan sources, propose questions, and sort them into categories. The categories become subtopics. Students join groups studying the subtopic of their choice. As a prelude to this stage, instructors may wish to show slides, a videotape or film, invite a visiting lecturer, visit a site, have students examine documents or scan books. The main questions to be asked at this stage are: What do we know about the problem or issue? What do we want to know?

Stage 2: Groups Plan Their Investigations. When the sub-topics have been identified, students sign up to be members of groups on the basis of their interest in a particular sub-topic. Instructors may have to negotiate with some students to ensure that groups do not become over or undersized, that cliques do not dominate particular groups, and that groups are otherwise heterogeneous.

Group members plan their investigations cooperatively: They decide what they will investigate, how they will go about it, and how they will divide the work among themselves. The procedural and organizational questions to be posed at this stage are: How will we find information about what we want to know? How will we divide the investigation into parts, and who will assume responsibility for which parts? What resources will we need to investigate this topic? Where will we find these resources?

Selection of particular questions to be investigated by students allows for the expression of individual preferences and talents. Not everyone has to do everything! All members have the responsibility to become thoroughly acquainted with all aspects of the groups' work, but no one individual needs to carry out the study of each and every problem dealt with by the entire group.

The instructor can, of course, identify some particular source or portion of a task that must be mastered by all of the students in the class. The entire class can always be assigned some task as required study for everyone apart from the topics investigated by the different groups. Such assignments are more likely to be accepted willingly by students within the context of their investigations than outside such a context, particularly if the instructor highlights the relevance of the assigned work for students' understanding of the topics they are investigating.

Instructors must perform the role of resource person in guiding students to appropriate resources. A wide variety of sources probably will have to be examined to fully investigate any genuine problem. Groups must be encouraged to identify for themselves sources of information regarding the topic at hand. On occasion, the group may discover gradually that its initial plan of the investigation was unrealistic or impractical, for whatever reason, and new planning must take place.

Stage 3: Groups Carry Out Their Investigations. This is typically the longest stage and may span any number of class sessions or may require a great deal of time to be spent outside of class. The question of time and group cooperation to implement its plan must be discussed in detail in each group.

Group members gather, organize, and analyze information from several sources. It may be advisable to have different students assume particular roles to make group organization efficient, such as: coordinator, recorder, secretary, etc., as the situation dictates.

Students pool their findings, interpret them as a group and form conclusions. Group members discuss their work in progress in order to exchange ideas and information, and to expand, clarify and integrate them. The more experience students have with Group Investigation, the more skilled they become in integrating all of the group members' contributions into the final group product.

Stage 4: Groups Plan Their Presentations. Group members determine the main ideas developed during their investigation. In this stage the groups plan how to present their findings by answering the following questions: Which of their findings does the group wish to present to the class? How will these findings be presented so the class will find them interesting?

Group representatives meet as a steering committee to coordinate plans for the final presentation to the class and consult with the instructor. Ideas for the presentation probably have been developing during the course of the investigation. Again, diverse talents can be given creative expression in the group presentation.

Stage 5: Groups Make Their Presentations. A schedule of presentations can be posted or copied and distributed to everyone. Presentations are made to the class in a variety of forms that emphasize class participation and minimize lectures by the presenting group. A few possibilities include setting up an exhibition, performing a skit or role-play, conducting an experiment, building a model, constructing a chart, or preparing a slide presentation.

Stage 6: Teacher and Students Evaluate Their Projects. The audience evaluates the clarity and appeal of each presentation, in addition to evaluating its intellectual and informational value for those who participated in the investigation and for the class as a whole. Students share feedback about their investigations and about their affective experiences. Teachers and students collaborate to evaluate individual, group and class wide learning. Evaluation can include a test, if the teacher feels it is necessary. Often students can be asked to contribute questions that will make up the test. However, the groups' presentations may well suffice as a solid basis for evaluating student learning.

TEACHING THE GROUP INVESTIGATION METHOD

One way of teaching students the Group Investigation method is to pose several major problems about the method itself and to have students propose specific questions for investigation. Students can then form study groups that focus their investigations on different features of the Group Investigation method.

Suggestions for problems that could be investigated are:
- What are the theoretical foundations of Group Investigation (G-I)? Students are asked to study, discuss and present the implications of the four main components of G-I: Investigation, Interaction, Interpretation and Intrinsic Motivation. How do these differ from prevailing pedagogical principles?
- What is the teacher's role or the students' role in each stage of G-I? What changes occur in these roles in contrast with expectations regarding those roles in traditional instruction?
- How should the learning task be designed?
- What are the effects of the learning task on group functioning? (Why will certain kinds of task design fail to engage the group while others succeed?)
- What is the role of students' cooperative planning in all stages of the G-I method? What is the contribution of students' planning to achieving the goals of G-I?

Findings from the investigation of G-I are discussed by a panel consisting of representatives from each of the study groups. This panel discussion can serve as the final presentation of the groups' work, or other presentations can be planned, depending on time, conditions and other constraints. Having students study the Group Investigation method is recommended when the goal is to have students become aware of the method by which they conduct their work. That is often an important goal not only for students of education, but for anyone who wishes to become acquainted with team research as practiced in many professional environments.

BIBLIOGRAPHY

Beebe, S. A. and Masterson, J. T. 1990. <u>Communicating in Small Groups</u>. Third Edition. Glenview, IL: Scott Foresman/Little, Brown Higher Ed.

Benedict, R. quoted in Maslow, A. 1971. <u>The Farther Reaches of Human Nature</u>. New York: Viking Press. 202.

Dewey, J. 1910. <u>How We Think</u>. New York: Heath.

Fisher, B. and Ellis, D. 1990. <u>Small Group Decision Making: Communication and the Group Process</u>. New York: McGraw-Hill.

Fruen, L. Spring 2000. "Outline for Consensus Decision Making" written for Speech 10 Collaborative Learning Class, De Anza College.

Galanes, G., Adams, K., and Brilhart, J. 2000. <u>Communicating in Groups</u>. Fourth Edition. Boston, Ma. McGraw-Hill.

Gordon, T. 1974. <u>Teacher Effectiveness Training</u>. New York: David McKay Co. Inc.

Hall, D. 1987. <u>To Read Literature</u>. New York: Holt, Rinehart and Winston.

Harrington, D. Fall 1995. "Outline for Four Group Skills" written for Speech 10, Collaborative Learning Class, De Anza College.

Lumsden, G. and Lumsden, D. 2000. <u>Communicating in Groups and Teams</u>. Third Edition. Belmont, Ca. Wadsworth.

Maslow, A. 1971. <u>The Farther Reaches of Human Nature</u>. New York: Viking Press.

Mead, M. 1966. <u>An Anthropologist at Work</u>. New York: Atherton Press. 351.

Pfeiffer, J. W. and Jones, J. E. 1981. <u>A Handbook of Structured Experiences for Human Relations Training</u>. San Diego, CA: University Associates Publishers and Consultants.

Sharan, Y. and Sharan, S. "Group Investigation in the University Classroom." a shortened version taken from: 1992. <u>Expanding Cooperative Learning Through Group Investigation</u>. New York, NY: Teachers College, Columbia University.

Wood, S. Fall 1994. "Example of a Collaborative Reading and Writing Project" found in "Cooperative Learning and College Teaching." Newsletter Vol. 5, #1.

PART IV *Public Communication*

INTRODUCTION

A common form of public communication is public speaking. It's safe to say that the prospect of **public speaking** -- having to stand up alone and make a planned presentation to an audience -- frightens just about everyone. To overcome this fear demands considerable assertiveness. The risks seem obvious enough:

I'll forget what I wanted to say.

My mind will go blank.

I won't have anything important to say.

I'll be boring.

People will disagree with my point of view.

I'll make a fool of myself.

Rather than take these risks, I may be passive and not be ready on the assigned day. Or I may drop the course! (That's about as passive a reaction as possible, but it does happen.) I may respond to this challenge aggressively, by treating the assignment as a joke, pretending that it's all really pretty silly anyway; it doesn't really matter that I'm unprepared. Perhaps I'll blame the course, the teacher, my classmates, my family. But with public communication, as with the other forms of communication, one must be willing to take appropriate risks in order to break out of the passive and aggressive ends of the continuum. Here too, one must choose to take necessary and appropriate risks in order to behave in an assertive manner.

The important thing to remember is that public speeches are delivered because there is a need. This is true for all situations, both formal and informal. Whether at a business meeting, staff briefing, college lecture, PTA meeting, professional conference, or city council session, you speak to achieve a goal. It is important to know exactly why you are speaking and what you hope to accomplish as you deliver your speech. You must consider the total interchange between you and your audience, not just what you do and say as you speak.

Two major Public Speaking assignments are described in this part of the workbook. The first is a Speech to Inform in which you will research a topic and organize the information you select into an interesting, coherent message for your audience. The second is a Speech to Persuade in which you will take a "stand" (a single point of view) from any part of your Speech to Inform and prepare a persuasive argument that explains and supports your "stand." So, both speeches come from the same general topic area -- only the purpose changes depending on whether you are informing or persuading your audience.

PUBLIC SPEAKING SUPPORT GROUPS

A Public Speaking Support Group is a Collaborative Group that will do just as the name implies. They will support you as you prepare, practice, and deliver public speeches. For example, the members of your Public Speaking Support Group will help you in several ways such as:

- brainstorm specific topics
- help with organization and planning of speeches
- critique the speech informally
- check your topic outline
- assist you with visual aids or any other needs during your speeches
- ask the first questions after the Informative Speech
- one will act as the Master/Mistress of Ceremonies for your Persuasive Speech

The purpose of the group is exactly as it sounds -- to support you! On the day of your speech delivery, you should not have to worry about anything but delivering the speech. Let the members of your support group take care of any other details for you.

TOPIC CHOICE AND RESEARCH

Considerations When Selecting a Topic

In general you will want to carefully consider many possible topics for your two public speeches. Think of topics that interest you. It is important that you think about your topic choice long enough to know that you can inform us about that topic and then persuade us in some specific way -- as described by your specific purpose of the speech.

Answering the following questions is a helpful way to begin the process of selecting a topic.

Am I interested in the topic? Do I have enough interest in this topic to spend time researching it so that I can feel confident about the information I prepare for the audience? Too often students will choose a speech topic because someone else is interested in that topic. For example, your roommate may be very interested in scuba diving and the state regulations regarding that sport. And you may enjoy discussing the topic with your roommate, but if you do not scuba dive yourself you probably are not interested enough in the topic to research it and use it for your speech topic. Rather, you need to think of a topic that is your own -- that you do care about and enthusiastically want to know more about.

Am I comfortable speaking about this topic? Is the language I will need to use to explain this topic, language that I am comfortable using? Too often students will choose a speech topic because it has to do with a subject which has some inherent "shock" value -- just because of the "shock" value. For example, sexually transmitted diseases is a topic for which many college students have a great deal of concern and interest. However, if you are not comfortable using the medical and technical language necessary to discuss this topic, then you should select a different topic altogether.

Will my research provide enough supporting information? Is there enough information available about this topic? Can I get a hold of the information in an appropriate amount of time so that it will be useful to me? As a speaker, it is necessary to make sure you will be able to get information for your speech. As soon as you can, check the topic to be sure your research will yield a good amount of information about your subject.

Workshop Activity: **Topic Selection - Brainstorming**

Answer the following questions to help you determine some possible topics for your public speeches.

What do you like to do in your spare time?
1.

2.

3.

What things interest you?
1.

2.

3.

What things in the current "world" situation would you like to change?
1.

2.

3.

What things are most important to you?
1.

2.

3.

What topics would you like to learn more about?
1.

2.

3.

What people or organizations interest you?
1.

2.

3.

Research Ideas

Traditional Sources - Check List

Below is a checklist of sources you might consider after you have selected your topic. Since it is always better to have more information than you will use in your speech, it is a good idea to think about how you might gather information from several of these sources.

THE LIBRARY
- Books
- Magazines
- Reference Materials

INTERVIEWS
- An expert in your topic area
- A person who has had an experience related to your topic area
- A person who is employed in an occupation that relates to your topic area
- An instructor who teaches classes related to your topic area

QUESTIONNAIRES/SURVEYS
- Audience Analysis of your own class
- Survey questions asked of a specific target group
- Survey questions asked randomly in other classes or groups

ELECTRONIC SEARCHES (if available at your public or school library)
- Infotrac
- Electric Library

NEWSPAPERS
- National newspapers such as The New York Times
- Local newspapers
- Your school newspaper

PAMPHLETS
- From organizations related to your topic
- From state or local agencies such as the Red Cross

TELEPHONE BOOK
- Check Listings for national, state or local agencies related to your topic
- Check listings for specific professionals who deal with your topic in some way

THE INTERNET
- Websites prepared by experts on the topic
- Information which can be appropriately documented by author, date (prove the source credible)

Forms of Supporting Information in the Speech

The use of supporting information makes the difference between a speech that is interesting rather than boring, persuasive rather than neutral, and one that makes sense rather than no sense to the audience. By using supporting information in a speech you can make the speech interesting, clear, and/or convincing. Supporting information is used to expand and emphasize each main point. It is not appropriate to state a main point or to make a persuasive claim without offering some form of support. Therefore, be sure to include supporting information throughout the speech always selecting interesting, clear, and convincing forms of support.

Select your supporting information carefully in order to find the most interesting, accurate, and believable material possible. Remember that supporting information adds the "flavor" to the point or claim. By giving the audience an example or a set of relevant statistics, the speaker makes the point or claim come alive for the listener. By the same token, when supporting information is presented it serves to help the listener believe the point or claim being made. If the speaker says that De Anza College is the largest community college in California the listener may or may not believe the statement. But, if the speaker supports the statement by showing a chart prepared by the State Board of Education listing the top five California colleges in terms of enrollment, then the listener can see the proof of the statement. There are many ways to elaborate the main ideas in your speech. Select a variety of support forms appropriate to your chosen topic, your individual speaking style, and your audience analysis.

STATISTICS: Prepared compilations of numbers that are often presented as percentages, comparisons or averages of numbers. When statistics are used in a speech they reinforce the point by providing numerical proof. Consider the following example from an outline on a speech about smoking written by Christina Typaldos.

I. By allowing minors to smoke, it can turn into a life long sentence of addiction.
   A. According to the FDA, almost 90% of adult smokers began before they reached their 18th birthday.
      1. According to our class survey, 55% of you have considered yourselves smokers at one time.
      2. Of those, 75% of you started underage.
   B. According to the FDA over 400,000 deaths occur yearly from smoking.
      1. According to Tobacco free Kids, 3,000 a day in the United Stated will become addicted to smoking.
      2. In addition, 1/3 of those minors will die prematurely due to smoking.

Notice how the statistics in the sub-points provide proof for the main point of minors' smoking addiction. When using statistics be careful not to overwhelm your audience with too many numbers. Often a visual aid is an effective means to let the audience see as well as hear a series of numbers.

EXAMPLES: Two types of examples that may be used as supporting information are real examples and hypothetical examples.

Real examples are reports of actual events that have happened. They are often presented in story or narrative form, but they can also be presented in a brief manner. In her speech about the Statue of Liberty, notice how Christina Typaldos used three specific real examples to support her point that the statue of Liberty has several symbols.

   C. The Statue of Liberty has several symbols that are actually visible to see according to Compton's Interactive Encyclopedia.
      1. For example, in Liberty's right hand she holds a tablet of law with the roman numerals that date July 4, 1776, our independence day.

2. Another example is a broken shackle representing tyranny that lies at her feet.
3. Finally, as a third example, the seven spikes in her crown represent freedom's light shining to the seven continents and the seven seas.

Notice how these specific examples add clarity and interest to the main point about symbols.

Hypothetical examples are invented by the speaker to help illustrate some point, but they are not genuine. As a speaker you are obligated to tell the audience when your example is hypothetical instead of real. Often speakers say something like "Picture this..." or "Imagine this..." to indicate the use of such an example. Use hypothetical examples when there is not a real example available but you can tell an example is needed in the speech. Or, create a hypothetical example to make a specific addition to the speech that specifically relates to your audience. Consider the Introduction of Lisa Golden's speech beginning on page 164. In the second paragraph she writes:

"Mr. and Mrs. Smith, a couple **I have invented for the speech**, both thought a dog would be so good to have. Mr. Smith imagined running on the beach with Fido, and playing Frisbee with him, and Mrs. Smith thought about hugging the precious little puppy. They both agreed on adopting a puppy for themselves, and since both Mr. and Mrs. Smith work, they thought it would be convenient to have a Dalmatian puppy delivered to their home via air mail express."

Observe her way of letting the listener know the example is hypothetical. Keep in mind that since hypothetical examples are made up, they cannot prove a point, but they can certainly help clarify one.

TESTIMONY: This form of supporting information includes statements from experts, peers, or personal experience. The statements are from those who have first hand experience and can offer a valid testimonial for the particular subject.

An example of Expert Testimony is used by Vickee Cermak in her persuasive speech beginning on page 196 when she quotes testimony given by a prominent cardiologist as the first sub-point to her first Main Point.

I. In order to prevent heart attack and strokes, we must begin to view Atherosclerosis as a disease of the young.
   A. According to Michael DeBakey M.D., a famous cardiologist, "Post-mortem studies carried out on young soldiers killed in the Korean War indicated that many of them had a significant degree of blockage due to Atherosclerosis of the coronary arteries by the time they were in their mid-twenties."

Notice how the speaker's point becomes more believable by the cardiologist's expert testimonial. Sometimes your own or other's experiences can be just as valid and important for the speech as an expert as long as the testimony is reliable and illustrates the point. In his speech about "Tinnitus" (ringing in the ears), Heath Kispaugh used his personal testimony as supporting information in his speech.

I. There are several symptoms which can be noticed when one has tinnitus.
   A. "In my own experience, I had ringing in my ears which stuck around permanently and has caused a lot of anxiety because it lead to loss of concentration and psychological distress."

Notice that this personal testimony adds to the clarity and understanding of the listener.

DEFINITION: A speaker should use definitions to tell the audience "here's what I mean." Define any terms or concepts from the speech that may be unfamiliar to the audience. Definitions should be simple and explicit. While dictionary definitions are quite common in speeches, a speaker may also define a term personally by explaining a concept in his/her own words. In his speech about medical care, Ken Brower uses the following definition of the "capitation fee model" within a sub-point.

C. One major threat to the quality care of patients is through the capitation fee model.
   1. In traditional fee-for-service insurance, doctors are paid each time they offer service to a patient.
   2. HMO's on the other hand, pay doctors a flat monthly fee such as $50 regardless of how often the doctor sees the patient and this fee **is called a capitation fee.**

It is clear that the definition is needed to clarify the term. Without the definition of the term "capitation fee model," the speaker runs the risk of confusing the audience.

POETRY: Poetry is a literary expression in which language is used in a concentrated blend of sound and imagery to create an emotional response; essentially rhythmic, it is usually metrical and frequently structured in stanzas.

Consider the way that this student uses Sara Teasdale's (1884-1933) poem The Long Hill to encourage audience members not to be distracted by life's adversaries in our journeys.

The Long Hill

I must have passed the crest a while ago
    And now I am going down-
Strange to have crossed the crest and not to know,
    But the brambles were always catching the hem of my gown.

All the morning I thought how proud I should be
    To stand there straight as a queen,
Wrapped in the wind and the sun with the world under me--
    But the air was dull, there was little I could have seen.

It was nearly level along the beaten track
    And the brambles caught in my gown--
But it's no use now to think of turning back,
    The rest of the way will be only going down.

SONG: A speaker may sing alone, or invite the audience to participate. "We Shall Overcome" is a popular song when members of a community come together to fight oppression and is often sung to form a sense of solidarity among group members.

Classroom speakers have written their own songs about everything from homelessness to the feeling of flying an airplane in order to help them elaborate their point of view.

NARRATIVE: Narration is also known as storytelling. It is different from example, in that it is generally more detailed, complete with a setting, character(s), plot, and perhaps dialogue. In his speech "The Rainbow Coalition," Jesse Jackson says, "I went to see Hubert Humphrey three days before he died. He had just called Richard Nixon from his dying bed, and many people wondered why. And I asked him. He said, 'Jesse, from this vantage point, with the sun setting in my life, all of the speeches, the political conventions, the crowds ands the great fights are behind me now. At a time like this, you are forced to deal with your irreducible essence, forced to grapple with that which is really important to you. And what I have concluded about life. Hubert Humphrey said, "When all is said and done, we must forgive each other and redeem each other, and move on." (Source: American Rhetoric from Roosevelt to Reagan)

DREAMS AND VISIONS: In some cultures, such as that of Native Americans, visions are considered more credible experiences than waking experiences. But perhaps the best example of dream as supporting information is Martin Luther King's famous speech "I Have a Dream", page 230 of this text, which uses a personal vision of the future to support his appeal to Americans to take part in the Civil Rights Movement.

FIGURES OF SPEECH: Through the creative use of language, a speaker can elaborate his or her ideas in a way that captures attention and motivates the audience toward action. Some examples include those you may recognize from your English composition class:

a. Alliteration--the repetition of initial sounds (consonants) of stressed syllables in neighboring words. For example, "Their policies divide the nation into the lucky and the left-out, the royalty and the rabble." (Source: American Rhetoric from Roosevelt to Reagan.) From Mario Cuomo's Keynote Address at the Democratic National Convention, 1984.

b. Antithesis--one thought is balanced with a contrasting thought in parallel arrangement of words or phrases. "Ask not what your country can do for you, ask what you can do for your country." Or, "We observe today not a victory of party but a celebration of freedom" both from John F. Kennedy Inaugural Address, 1961. Source: (http://www.tamu.edu/scom/pres/speeches/jfkinaug.html)

c. Anaphora and Repetition--the repetition of a word or expression at the beginning of successive phrases. Such as Lincoln's, "...we cannot dedicate--we cannot consecrate--we cannot hallow--this ground." (from The Gettysburg Address) Or, "We are a people in a quandary about the present. We are a people in search of our future. We are a people in search of a national community. We are a people trying not only to solve the problem of the present; unemployment, inflation.... but we are attempting to fulfill our national purpose; to create and sustain a society in which all of us are equal." Barbara C. Jordan, 1976 Democratic Convention Keynote Address (Source: American Rhetoric from Roosevelt to Reagan.)

d. Metaphor--a word or phrase literally denoting one object is applied to another, suggesting an analogy. One effective example form King's "I Have a Dream" speech is the "bad check" metaphor that he carries through several paragraphs.

e. Personification--a type of metaphor in which distinctive human characteristics, for example, emotions, are attributed to an animal, object, or idea. "Fate frowned on her endeavors."

f. Imagery--elements of rhetoric used to evoke mental images, not only visual, but of sensation and emotion as well. An example comes from the Introduction of Sarah Jensen's speech "Standing Face to Face with Poverty" which begins on page 199. "My heart was pounding as I knocked on the door to the one-roomed shack in the heart of Mexico's dump. I was excited that I had the opportunity to bring food to a poor family, but most of my anxiety stemmed from the fact that once the door opened, I knew I'd be standing face to face with poverty. As a tiny girl opened the door to her shack, my eyes awakened to the reality of poverty. She looked at me, startled to see a blond "gringa" at her door, but smiled as I handed her the food. As she yelled for her momma to come, I peeked into the small house, seeing temporary beds set up all over the dirt floor. The smells were unmistakable. I had gotten a true glimpse of poverty."

PROVERB: Proverbs are concise sayings that represent cultural truths. Consider this African proverb (Ghana): "If you educate a man, you educate an individual, but if you educate a woman, you educate a family (nation)." Through exaggeration this proverb explains the importance of women in raising a child and acknowledges that once we know the value of education for men, we should allow women to have equal access.

AUDIENCE PARTICIPATION: It may be appropriate to invite the audience to respond during a speaker's presentation. Audience participation can include several forms, such as:

    a.   Testimonial. You may arrange with an audience member to offer an example from his or her life experience that relates to your main idea. For example, "Gianna, I know you have studied abroad, would you like to tell us about your experiences in Florence, Italy?" It is usually too risky for beginning speakers to use this technique without rehearsing with your classmate in advance of the presentation.

    b.   Call and Response. This is an opportunity for audience members to join in the rhythm of an address as a means of affirmation to the speaker. It is a common strategy in African-American rhetoric.

AUDIO-VISUAL AIDS: This method of elaboration includes photographs, charts, graphs, slides, videotapes and tape recordings. For example, "This selection by Nina Simone exemplifies the style of jazz I have explained in my speech."

Checking your Research

It is the responsibility of the speaker to verify all of the information presented to the audience in a speech. To verify information means to establish the credibility of the source, and then to be prepared to give credit to the source of the information during the speech.

CREDIBILITY: Check the credibility of your sources by asking the following:
Who is the source of this information?

Why is this source appropriate for this information?

How was this information gathered, reported?

Is this a believable source of information?

Is the source of information biased in some way?

How recent is the information? Is it in an appropriate time frame to be relevant?

PLAGIARISM: As a speaker, you must never plagiarize information in a speech. You must be very careful that every time during the speech you use information directly from one of your sources of information, that you give the credit to your information source in the speech. You are responsible to give credit to your information sources whether you are directly quoting from the source, or whether you are paraphrasing from the source.

Example of a Direct Quotation: According to Edwina Stoll, the Instructor of Record for this class, "There are two speeches formed out of one general topic area due in this class."

Example of Paraphrased Information: When I talked to our instructor, Edwina, she said we would have two speeches due in this class on the same topic.

WRITING THE SPEECH

Identifying the Purpose of the Speech

The first three steps in the process of speech preparation are generally considered to be the most important steps because they not only give you the specific direction of your speech but also suggest the main points for your speech. These three steps will provide you with the overall framework for your speech.

Step 1: The General Purpose. This broad statement indicates your overall intention or goal for the speech. Examples of General Purpose Statements are "To Inform" or "To Persuade."

Step 2: The Specific Purpose. This statement is an indication of the desired outcome you seek from the audience. It is always written with the audience in mind. The Specific Purpose is written for the speaker. It is usually not included in the delivery of the speech to the audience. Rather, it aids the speaker in focusing on the desired outcome of the speech.

Step 3: The Thesis Statement. The thesis statement for a Speech to Inform will show the way you have focused or narrowed your topic so that it will satisfy the general and the specific purpose of the speech. The thesis statement has two goals: first, it introduces the focused topic to the audience; and, second, it is a preview of the Main Points that will be covered in the body of the speech. The speaker always delivers the thesis statement to the audience during the speech.

The thesis statement for a Speech to Persuade is called a Proposition. The persuasive speech is written to have an effect on the members of the audience. The speaker may want to *stimulate* the audience, so they think more about the topic, or to *convince* the audience about some point of view, or the speaker may want to *actuate* the audience so that they literally do something as a result of the speech.

Example: Three Steps to identify the purpose of a Speech to Inform using the topic "Small Claims Court."

GENERAL PURPOSE: To Inform

SPECIFIC PURPOSE: After listening to this speech the audience will be informed of the three-step process for taking a claim to Small Claims Court.

THESIS STATEMENT: Three major steps to following through a small claims court case are: one, determining that you have a case; two, preparing your case for court; and three, actually going to court.

Workshop Activity: **Writing Specific Purpose and Thesis for Speech to Inform**

       Members of the support group will work together for this activity in which you will practice turning a speech "topic idea" into the Specific Purpose and Thesis Statement for a Speech to Inform. Fill in the missing steps for the following hypothetical speeches.

#1   TOPIC: DPAHC (Durable Power of Attorney for Health Care)

        GENERAL PURPOSE:

        SPECIFIC PURPOSE:

        THESIS STATEMENT: In order to insure that your wishes regarding your medical care will be respected by utilizing a DPAHC, you must first, decide who you would choose to be your representative or "agent"; second, understand the procedure that is necessary to secure a DPAHC; and third, clearly understand the limitations that exist when using this type of documentation.

#2   TOPIC: College Education in California

        GENERAL PURPOSE:

        SPECIFIC PURPOSE: After listening to this speech audience members will be informed of three types of college education programs that are available in California.

        THESIS STATEMENT:

#3   TOPIC: Seat Belts

        GENERAL PURPOSE: To Inform

        SPECIFIC PURPOSE:

        THESIS STATEMENT:

Workshop Activity: Writing Specific Purpose and Thesis for Speech to Persuade

    Members of the support group will work together for this activity in which you will practice turning a speech "topic idea" into the General Purpose, Specific Purpose, and Thesis Statement (now called a Proposition), and Main Points for a Speech to Persuade.

#1   TOPIC: Collaborative Learning

       GENERAL PURPOSE:

       SPECIFIC PURPOSE:

       PROPOSITION: The Collaborative Learning Methodology should be used in more classes on campus because it encourages more student participation in class and it discourages students from dropping the class.

       MAIN POINTS:

       I.

       II.

#2   TOPIC: Tutoring high school students

       GENERAL PURPOSE:

       SPECIFIC PURPOSE: After listening to this speech the audience will be persuaded to volunteer to tutor speech communication skills to high school students.

       PROPOSITION:

       MAIN POINTS:

       I.

       II.

       III.

The Speech Outline

A full sentence outline is used when writing speeches in order to allow the speaker to frame the information of the speech into full complete sentences at least one time before delivering the speech to the audience. The following is the information about each of the parts of a full sentence outline written in correct outline form. These outlining instructions are adapted from "Outlining Instructions," by Gary Miller. (Reprinted with permission.)

Model: **Full Sentence Outline Form**

INTRODUCTION

The speech outline begins with an INTRODUCTION that provides the audience with a reason to listen to the speech. The Introduction to a speech contains three parts: the Attention Device, the Speaker's Credibility Statement, and the Thesis Statement. The introduction is written in full prose style and is labeled. The first part of the introduction called the attention device is selected for the purpose of getting the audience listening to the speaker. It should be related to the speech, but it should not give away the specific purpose of the speech just yet. There are several types of attention devices discussed on page 149. The speaker should select one of these devices that would appropriately introduce the speech topic. Next in the introduction, the speaker needs to establish credibility with the audience. To establish credibility, the speaker should confirm for the audience that the topic has been carefully researched and the message specifically prepared for this audience. In this segment of the introduction the audience members will learn shy the speaker selected the particular topic. Sometimes topics are selected because the speaker has some special expertise. Other times, topics are selected because the speaker has an interest in the topic and wants to learn more about it through the research. Whatever the reason for the topic choice, it is important that the speaker share it with the audience. The third part of the introduction is the thesis.

The THESIS is a concise statement that tells the point of the speech (called the purpose) and identifies the way the speaker will cover or explain the point (called the preview). The thesis statement is written in precise language in one or two sentences and is delivered as it was written. It is important that the speaker emphasize the thesis as it is delivered because it provides an overview of the speech for the audience. In other words, the thesis provides a road map so the audience knows what they can expect to learn during the speech.

Follow these RULES when writing the thesis.
1. The thesis is written in one or two declarative sentence(s) that epitomize the entire speech.
2. The first part of the thesis lets the audience know the point of the speech and is called the purpose.
3. The second part of the thesis lists each of the main points (shown as roman numerals in the full sentence outline) to be covered in the speech in the same order in which they will be discussed by the speaker and thus, is called the preview.
4. The thesis must be labeled in the full sentence outline.
5. The thesis statement for a persuasive speech is called a proposition.

BODY (The BODY of the outline must be labeled)

I. The main points, sub-points, and sub sub-points must be stated in complete declarative sentences.

    A. Full declarative sentences are required in order that your meaning will be clear to yourself and to me as I read your outline.

    B. Use only one sentence per outline symbol.

C. Do not use questions, words, or phrases in stating main points, sub-points, and sub sub-points in the outline.

II. The points of the outlined body must be properly subordinated.

   A. Main points should develop, support, or explain the thesis or proposition.

   B. Sub-points should support, develop, explain, and clarify the main points.

   C. Sub sub-points will develop, support, explain, and clarify the sub-points.

   D. Subordination of main and sub-points in the outline must be made evident by proper indentation.

III. Outline symbols must be consistent with these rules.

   A. Use Roman Numerals for main points.

   B. Use Upper Case Letters for sub-points.

   C. Use Arabic Numbers for sub sub-points.

   D. Use Lower Case Letters for sub sub sub-points.

   E. Use indentations to indicate the relationship between coordination and subordination of ideas.

   F. The common form is shown in the following example.

   I.
      A.
         1.
         2.
      B.
         1.
         2.
            a.
            b.
   II.
      A.
      B.

IV. In the body of the outline you should provide for an adequate number of developmental or support materials. (Refer to page 134 for ideas about how to amplify and explain your main points.)

    A. Your subject must be narrow enough to permit amplification of each point.

    B. There are several ways to develop or support material.

        1. Statistics, figures, or numbers are often used and should be accompanied with use of association and/or comparison.

        2. Use analogy, comparison, and contrast for showing similarities and differences.

        3. Use quotations when presenting testimony from authority.

        4. Illustrations can further explain a point.

    C. Anecdotes can personalize and highlight a point.

    D. Always cite sources within the body of the outline.

CONCLUSION

An outline, to be complete, will include a CONCLUSION that is written in full prose style and properly labeled. The conclusion has three parts: Summary, Audience Closure, and Clincher. The conclusion summary should summarize the main points of the speech. The conclusion audience closure will give the speech a sense of finality for the audience. Often this section of the conclusion refers back to the introduction. The last sentence of the conclusion is the clincher. A simple way to use a clincher is to have it refer back to the attention device of the introduction or to think of it as one last memorable thought for the audience to remember. The conclusion must not introduce new information. The conclusion should be approximately the same length as the Introduction.

BIBLIOGRAPHY

Every outline must have a BIBLIOGRAPHY.

- The bibliography indicates the sources from which you obtained information for the speech.

- Research could include personal experience, general reading, observation, interviews, and library and Internet research.

- It is not acceptable to draw entirely from your own experience, observation, or knowledge for your speech, as outside research is a requirement of the assignment.

- If you have obtained information from sources in addition to your own experience and knowledge, indicate this by using the correct bibliography form.

- The Bibliography will always include Citations for every source used.

- The Bibliography will be organized alphabetically by the author's last name. If no author is listed, it is shown by "_____" and the citation is placed at the end of the alphabetical list.

- The Bibliography will often include your own written Annotation for each Citation of a source.

AUDIO/VISUAL AIDS

Provide a list of the audio/visual aids to be used during the speech.

Bibliographic Citations

Follow these general guidelines when writing your bibliography.

1. Organize the entries alphabetically by the last name of the author. If your source has "no author," show that by using seven underlines (_____.) before listing the other information. Listings with no author come at the end of the bibliography and are organized by the first word of the title of the source.
2. When the written listing is longer than one typed line, then each subsequent line should be indented under the first line by seven spaces.
3. If your source was found using the Internet, be sure that you list the author or organization that is responsible for the source so that you can give it the appropriate credit. You may have to search through the source a bit to find this information. The specific address of the Internet site must also be included.
4. As you read through the variety of sources listed below as examples, note that at the end of each example we have named the type of example in parenthesis (i.e. books, interview, etc.). When you write your bibliography you should not include the listing in parenthesis.

BIBLIOGRAPHY

Burby, R. J. Communicating With People. Menlo Park: Addison-Wesley Publishing Co. 1970. (Book)

Dewey, R. (n.d./1996). APA Publication Manual Crib Sheet. Psych Web by Russ Dewey [WWW document]. URL http://www.gasou.edu/psychweb/tipsheet/apacrib.html (Internet source including name of author and specific website)

Koile, E. Listening As a Way of Becoming. Texas, Calibre, 1999. (Book)

Montgomery, R. L. "Are You a Good Listener?" Nation's Business. Oct. 1981. Vol. 12. 65-68. (Article in a Magazine)

Walker, T., Ph.D. Interview concerning speaking skills of Public Speaking Teachers. May 1, 2001. San Jose, California. (Interview)

Youngblood, J. "Speech Communication Courses in Community College." Survey. Taken May 23, 1999 in a speech class containing 28 students. (Survey in a class)

_____. "Speak and Find Success." Pamphlet. Speech Association of America. January 1998. (Pamphlet without an author)

_____. "Your Own Voice." Produced by NBC and aired September 15, 2000 on the national network. (Television Documentary with no stated author).

Attention Device and Clincher

Based on ideas from Melinda Williams, Williams Baptist College, Walnut Ridge, Arkansas. (Reprinted with permission.)

Effective public speeches begin and end with memorable statements known as the Attention Device for the Introduction and the Clincher for the Conclusion. Here are a series of definitions and examples so that you can select the ones that will be most useful for your speech topic and impressive to your audience.

NOTE: The Attention Device begins the Introduction of the speech and the Clincher ends the Conclusion of the speech.

RHETORICAL QUESTIONS: A question for the audience to ponder, not answer. Be careful that this does not become a "black hole," sucking in beginning speakers because they cannot create a more effective introduction or conclusion. Usually it is a good idea to use rhetorical questions in a series of two or three so they really can serve as an *attention device*. For example, if your topic is photography, you might ask: "Have you been frustrated when pictures you took didn't turn out? Does your `One-Hour' photo lab post your photographs as examples of what **not** to do?"

ILLUSTRATION or ANECDOTE: A real or hypothetical story; it is the speaker's obligation to tell if the story is not real.

STARTLING STATEMENT: Statistics work very well for statements that provide the audience with something to consider. Remember to cite the source as you state your facts.

QUOTATION: It is important to cite the source of a quote. For example, if you use the line "Ask not what your country can do for you; ask what you can do for your country.", be sure to credit John Kennedy, who spoke the line in his Inaugural Address.

HUMOR: Everyone likes a good joke, but it does need to be funny, be pertinent to the speech, and the speaker needs to be able to handle the reaction of the audience. Be careful of tasteless, off-color, or prejudicial humor; no one finds those funny, as all humor is culture-bound. Be sure that your joke does not alienate audience members who do not share the same common culture with you. Also, do not let it be a crutch; all speeches do not have to begin with a joke. And finally, if you do not usually tell jokes, it is probably better to avoid telling a joke to begin your speech.

ACTION: Certain speeches might lend themselves to begin or end with an action. For example, an informative speech on sign language could easily begin and end with actual demonstrations of sign language to accompany the spoken language. You might also create a skit or dramatization that involves others in the class.

AUDIO/VISUAL AID: Use a video clip, some photography, or music. Limit the audio/visual aid to less than 30 seconds as this counts as part of your speaking time.

PRACTICING YOUR SPEECH DELIVERY

As the diagram below indicates, your speech delivery style should be "extemporaneous." An extemporaneous delivery is very carefully prepared and practiced beforehand so that it sounds spontaneous, yet organized, to the audience. Extemporaneous delivery allows for the use of note cards if the speaker wishes to use them. An extemporaneous delivery is also a natural type of delivery. The speaker concentrates on communicating with the audience -- on making sure that every member of the audience can hear and understand the speech. The speaker does this by being him/herself during the delivery of the speech rather than trying to be like someone else.

SPEECH DELIVERY STYLE

	IMPROMPTU	EXTEMPORANEOUS	VERBATIM
	"Off the top of your head"	*Planned, Practiced Seems Spontaneous,*	*Memorized or Read Word for Word*
SMALL GROUP	**SEMINAR**	**SYMPOSIUM, PANEL**	
PUBLIC SPEAKING		**SPEECH TO INFORM SPEECH TO PERSUADE**	

We asked Melinda Williams, who uses our workbook in her classes at Williams Baptist College, to give us suggestions for this edition of the workbook. We liked her ideas about speech delivery so much that we have included them in their entirety. (Reprinted with permission.)

Two myths exist with beginning speakers concerning the delivery of a speech: one is that you should pick a point on the back wall and talk to it during the speech; the other is rather than looking into the audience's eyes, you should look at the top of their heads during the speech (which means the speaker is looking toward but not at the audience). Practicing either of these myths will cause one of two things to happen during a performance: people will either turn around to see what is on the back wall that the speaker keeps staring at, or will gracefully excuse themselves to go to the restroom to fix their hair (obviously something is wrong or the speaker wouldn't be staring at the top of their head).

Delivery is important to a speaker. Not only does it enhance the work spent preparing the speech, but it also adds to the speaker's credibility and encourages the audience's attention and retention. The goal of all types of communication discussed in this workbook is assertiveness. Assertiveness in delivery of a speech shows confidence from the speaker, contact with the audience, and control of the speaking situation.

Speakers learn to develop a style of their own: Jesse Jackson uses a call and response technique in his speaking delivery. Former President Bill Clinton points, but not with his index finger, with his thumb. The most important quality of a speaker's delivery is that it fits the speaker; it is natural and comfortable to them. The speaker may choose to shout and slap the podium, cheer and chant, or jest and joke, just so long as it fits one's personality.

Two aspects of delivery must be considered: verbal and non-verbal behavior. The verbal behavior of a speaker concerns how the voice is used, including the pitch (highness or lowness of voice), rate (speed of delivering words and pauses), volume, projection (direction the voice is pointed), pronunciation (saying the words correctly), and articulation (forming the correct vowel and consonant sounds). The most important elements of a speaker's verbal behavior are variety and energy. We use variety in normal conversations: pitches rise when excited or at the end of a question; rate is slowed for important statements; volume is raised for attention. What a speaker must learn to do is utilize the same verbal behavior in public speeches as in normal conversation.

The speaker must also learn how to use the body's reaction to "stage fright" in developing energy in the delivery of a speech. Energy is pumping throughout the speaker's body as a reaction to the fear he is facing. By learning to control the body's reaction through focusing that energy into the speech, the speaker comes out with a dynamic delivery.

The speaker must learn to control both the verbal and non-verbal behaviors in a speech. One must always be aware of what one's body is doing and fit the non-verbal behavior with the content of the speech. The body movements of a speaker should not be distracting, such as a twitch, fondling loose change in a pocket, smacking lips before words, or standing with one's weight all on a single foot. Speakers should not force themselves to conform to a standard way to stand during a speech; a standard way does not exist except for what is right for the speaker, showing confidence and not distracting the audience.

Some important elements of non-verbal behavior that should be stressed are facial expressions, eye contact, and posture. Facial expressions are mirrors of how the speaker feels about himself, his audience, and his subject. If the speaker looks as though someone is standing behind him forcing him to speak at gunpoint, the audience senses this discomfort and feels uncomfortable, too. The face should enhance the message and the eyes should direct the audience to the speaker. As a rule, eye contact usually puts a speaker more in control of one's fear, allowing more effective communication with the audience by reading their feedback and adjusting the delivery.

Posture is also an important element of non-verbal behavior since it not only reflects a speaker's confidence, but also helps in breathing and vocal control. Other aspects of non-verbal behavior are important in the delivery of a speech; movement, gestures, appearance, and use of space, all can be determined by the speaker's personality and taste, the audience, and the occasion of the speech.

The theatre world refers to a performer's "charisma" when examining how one plays an audience. Speakers need charisma, too, for a delivery that is natural, comfortable, and gives the appearance of confidence. At times it is difficult to feel confident when palms are sweating, knees are knocking, and stomachs are turning, but the speaker should always control the verbal and non-verbal behavior in a speech to give the appearance of confidence.

The best way to choose an appropriate delivery is for the speaker to consider one's own tastes, personality, and comfort level, as well as the audience, and the occasion of the speech. Experience will teach a speaker how to read an audience's feedback and determine the difference between an uncomfortable message and an uncomfortable seat.

The Four-Day Practice Plan

Extemporaneous Delivery of speeches means that you will want to concentrate on communicating with the audience rather than speaking at the audience. As a general rule, never read or memorize your speech because your delivery will then tend to not be communicative but rather stilted.

What follows is a "Four Day Plan" for practicing speeches that has been tested by students. In this plan, the speaker has the Full Sentence Outline for the speech prepared four days before the speech is due which will allow enough time to practice the actual speech delivery. To prepare for speech delivery, practice the speech several times each day pairing down the number of note cards you need as you progress.

151

Day 1: Full Sentence Outline.
   FOUR DAYS BEFORE SPEECH: Practice using your Full Sentence Outline. Practice the speech out loud and standing up. Pay particular attention to learning the Introduction, Thesis, Main Points, and the Conclusion. Those four parts of the speech should be delivered while giving as much eye contact to the audience as possible.

Day 2: As Many Note Cards as you need.
   THREE DAYS BEFORE SPEECH: Begin this practice day by writing out as many note cards as you need to feel comfortable to make the transition between the full sentence outline and the note cards. As you practice pay particular attention to the four parts of the speech and to emphasizing your transitions between each part. Practice out loud and standing up. Check the time of your delivery and make any adjustment to meet the time limit for the speech.

Day 3: Maximum of Five Note Cards.
   TWO DAYS BEFORE SPEECH: Begin this practice day by writing notes on five or fewer note cards. Using only five note cards will insure that you do deliver the speech in an extemporaneous manner and that you give yourself the maximum opportunity to communicate and keep consistent eye contact with the audience.

Day 4: Polishing the Delivery.
   ONE-DAY BEFORE SPEECH: By this time you will know the speech very well. Concentrate on giving maximum eye contact to the audience as you practice your speech out loud and standing up. Emphasize all of the parts of the speech and be as communicative as possible.

Tips for Dealing with Speech Anxiety or Stage Fright

   It is important to realize that some nervousness is normal when you are going to deliver a public speech. Even the best speakers get a bit nervous before facing an audience. The following suggestions should help you cope with your own anxiety or fear. If you find that in spite of these suggestions you are still experiencing a high degree of anxiety, meet with your instructor to discuss the topic further.

1. All of the experts agree that <u>preparation</u> is the best strategy you can use to reduce your anxiety toward public speaking. <u>Prepare</u> by selecting a topic you care about and have a genuine interest in exploring with us in two different ways (inform and persuade). <u>Prepare</u> by doing careful research so you find interesting supporting information. <u>Prepare</u> by bouncing ideas off of members of your support group. <u>Prepare</u> by following the "practice plan." And, <u>prepare</u> in any other way(s) that will be most helpful and relaxing to you -- the speaker.

2. Understand the physiology of speech anxiety. The medical profession has determined that it is much the same as feeling excited in that it may increase your heart rate, cause your hands to feel clammy or cause some shaking in the hands or legs.

3. Dealing with this anxiety is a challenge that faces just about all speakers, both beginner and experienced. You are not alone in that respect, and this knowledge can make the experience less formidable <u>and can transform your anxiety into positive energy</u>, just as an athlete feels "up" for a big game. One way to accomplish this is to replace any negative self-talk with positive statements. You have already spoken to this audience during earlier less formal class presentations so let those accomplishments remind you that you can speak to this audience successfully.

4. Practice delivering the speech out loud. Use the Four Day Practice method described on the previous page. This method will allow you plenty of time to become comfortable with your speech content.

5. Face the audience. Do not turn your back to people, even when using a visual aid. Be conscious of audience awareness. Establish adequate eye contact with several members of your audience. Avoid looking only at one person throughout the speech.

6. Be aware of your body language: how you stand and move in front of the audience. Try not to slouch or pace. Do not be afraid to move around, if this is appropriate. (For example, closer to the group if you are asking for questions, back toward a visual aid, when you want to focus attention to it.) Begin in the "ready position" not with your hands in your pockets or clasped in front or back of the body. Your legs and shoulders should be parallel, knees loose, and your arms at your sides.

7. Most people feel anxiety -- to one degree or another -- when speaking before a group. And since every student in this class will also be giving a speech to the class, you will find a great deal of understanding and support from the members of the audience.

8. Visualize. See yourself in front of your class audience -- and visualize yourself speaking assertively/successfully! This type of a Self-Fulfilling Prophecy is an important factor in public speaking.

9. Talk about your feelings of nervousness with your support group. Sharing your feelings will help you to put them in better perspective -- and you will no doubt learn that others in your support group have some of the same feelings. Practice together if possible and make use of feedback you receive in advance.

10. Reframe the audience's role in the speech situation. See the speech as an opportunity to present a message to individuals, rather than as a formal occasion to *perform* as an actor or actress. Even when you are in complete control of what you are saying, a conversational style of delivery is the most appropriate. (This is called Extemporaneous style.) An extemporaneous delivery style will make the audience feel your message is more personally oriented for them. Remember, the audience wants to see you succeed. They are not here to count mistakes.

11. Use visual aids. They tend to help you feel more organized and prepared. They also will hold the audience's attention and help them understand the information you are discussing in the speech. For more information about visual aids see below.

12. Practice with someone timing you so that timing signals given during the speech will not surprise or panic you. You can adjust the pace of your speech if necessary. If timing is a problem, have a support group member give you signals to speed up or slow down during practice sessions and the actual speech.

13. It is important to not forego sleep to practice the speech. Rest. Eat something. Do not change your daily routine on a speech day.

Ideas for Using Visual/Audio Aids

Contributed by Susan Endter, De Anza College. (Reprinted with permission.)

Visual/Audio Aids are valuable in helping the audience comprehend and retain information. Some common types of these aids include: charts, graphs, and other pictorial representations; movies, slides, and projections; music or sounds; and handouts. Such aids should be carefully prepared and integrated into the message.

PREPARATION OF VISUAL/AUDIO AIDS

1. Should be large enough or loud enough to be seen or heard easily.

2. Charts, graphs, and drawings should use broad lines and colors that are vivid and contrasting. Be creative.

3. Visual Aids should be simple, clear, and easily understood without sacrificing accuracy.

4. Visual Aids should be easy to handle.

5. Consider how you will display and visual. Bring tape!

6. The Font for an overhead transparency should be 3 times the regular size to be easily projected. Use no more than two fonts per transparency for easy reading by the audience.

USE OF VISUAL/AUDIO AIDS

1. The introduction of the visual/audio aid into the message should be carefully planned and thoroughly rehearsed. Do not let the aid disrupt your delivery.

2. Introduce the aids into the flow of information smoothly and naturally.

3. Display an object so that it can be seen easily by all members of the audience, and do not obstruct it from view during your delivery. Keep the commentary going.

4. Talk to the audience about the object being displayed. Do not talk to your visual aid.

5. Put away or cover the device or object when it is not in use.

6. Do not pass items among an audience. This creates too much of a distraction.

7. Cite your source when playing or showing the aid. Even if the source is printed on a visual aid, you need to verbally cite it within the speech.

8. Save handouts for the end of the speech. To hand them out during the speech is too noisy and distracting.

Student Request Form: Speech Dates

REQUEST FOR SPEAKING DATES FOR INFORMATIVE SPEECH

NAME_____

Indicate the days you prefer by writing "1st," "2nd," and "3rd," or "no preference."

	Monday	**Tuesday**	**Wednesday**	**Thursday**	**Friday**
DATES	_____	_____	_____	_____	_____
DATES	_____	_____	_____	_____	_____
DATES	_____	_____	_____	_____	_____

No Preference _____

REQUEST FOR SPEAKING DATES FOR PERSUASIVE SPEECH

NAME_____

Indicate the days you prefer by writing "1st," "2nd," and "3rd," or "no preference."

	Monday	**Tuesday**	**Wednesday**	**Thursday**	**Friday**
DATES	_____	_____	_____	_____	_____
DATES	_____	_____	_____	_____	_____
DATES	_____	_____	_____	_____	_____

No Preference _____

THE SPEECH TO INFORM

Assignment Specifics

PURPOSE:

1. To give you experience in researching, organizing, outlining, practicing and presenting dynamic information to the audience.

2. To prepare a speech which will hold the audience's interest and insure their full understanding through the use of clear Main Points that are followed by thorough Supporting Information.

REQUIREMENTS:

1. A 5 to 7 minute speech which will be timed and penalized if over or under the required time limit

2. Extemporaneous Style (planned, practiced, and seemingly spontaneous)

3. Speaker may take only note cards and audio/visual aids to the front of the room

4. Visual Aids Required -- in a rare instance this may be waived

5. Three sources of information which are cited in the speech

6. Supporting Information for each main point

7. Working outlines presented to Support Group prior to speech

8. Full sentence outline and bibliography due on day speech is presented to class

9. After speech delivery, 3 minutes are allotted for questions from audience (members of support group are expected to begin the questions). This time is not part of your speech time or your speech grade.

10. Videotape -- Speaker provides a personal videotape to the camera operator prior to the speech.

Examples: **Full Sentence Outlines for Speeches to Inform**

"STATUE OF LIBERTY"

By Christina Typaldos
(Reprinted with permission.)

INTRODUCTION

Do you know what the nation's most recognizable sign of freedom next to the American Flag is? "It is the world's most celebrated symbol of American Freedom and democracy" according to author's Dillion and Kotler in The Statue Of Liberty Revisited. It shows the world that our country is founded on, what we fought the revolution for, our freedom. Does "Liberty Enlightening The World," sound familiar? It is what the people called "The Statue of Liberty" in 1886. We know the Statue of Liberty stands for our freedom, but the statue did not appear over night. Someone had to think of the concept of making this statue. Well, tonight I am not going to explain how the Statue of Liberty represents our freedom, but rather the history of the making of the statue so that all of us may enjoy a greater understanding of this national monument.

THESIS

There are three major parts in understanding how the Statue of Liberty came to stand tall at Liberty Island: the idea behind the statue, the design and symbolic meaning, and how it was moved to the island and had to wait for pedestal.

BODY

I. The idea of a monument to be built to commemorate American Independence came from Edourd Rene Laboulaye, a professor and leading French legal scholar, at a dinner party, according to the Statue of Liberty sponsored by PBS.

   A. Laboulaye urged his friend, Frederic Auguste Bartholdi, to build the monument and to take a trip to the United States to find a location for the statue and to meet the people.

      1. When Bartholdi arrived, the first sight he saw was Bedloe's Island, now called Liberty Island, and he knew he wanted the statue to stand there, because it would be the first sight that all immigrants would see.

      2. According to The Statue of Liberty sponsored by A&E, Bartholdi designed the outside of the statue with enough copper to press 30 million pennies.

         a. According to Ed Cohen, a restoration engineer, the statue was going to be solid with boxes of sand to give it stability by Eugene Emmanuel Viollet-le-Duc.

         b. A new engineer, Alexandre Gustave Eiffel, came to replace Viollet-le-Due and had a new concept to the world, of making an iron tower like a dressmakers dummy.

   B. Laboulaye organized and served as a chairman of the Franco-American Union, which was the campaign to build the statue, according to the Statue of Liberty video sponsored by PBS.

(TRANSITION: Now that we know more about how the idea of building the statue came about, we can move onto the design and symbolic meanings of the statue.)

II. Bartholdi, designed the Statue of Liberty in France calling her "My American" and included many symbolic meanings none of which were symbols of power, but symbols of faith, according to The Statue of Liberty video sponsored by A&E.

    A. The first step in the design of the statue is what she would look like, which came from two influences.

        1. According to author Oscar Handlin, in his Newsweek article "The Statue of Liberty," Bartholdi turned to "his mother, a tall, powerful, a sheltering presence ever offering a refuge for those in need."

        2. Bartholdi then turned to his mistress for the shape of the body.

    B. According to "Statue of Liberty" a Web Site put out by the National Park Service, the first real symbol is that the statue was a gift from the French people to the American people showing the friendship among the two countries.

    C. The Statue of Liberty has several symbols that are actually visible to see according to Compton's Interactive Encyclopedia.

        1. For example, in Liberty's right hand she holds a tablet of law with the roman numerals that date July 4, 1776, our independence day.

        2. Another example is a broken shackle representing tyranny that lies at her feet.

        3. Finally, as a third example, the seven spikes in her crown represent freedom's light shining to the seven continents and the seven seas.

(TRANSITION: Now that the Statue of Liberty had been created, she was ready to be moved to America.)

III. Bringing the Statue to America dealt with transportation problems and waiting for the pedestal, which created a great controversy here in America, according to Handlin.

    A. The Statue of Liberty was put into more than 300 pieces so it could cross the ocean, requiring almost 200 ships to carry all the pieces.

    B. After the arrival of the Statue of Liberty, it took more than four weeks to unload all of the pieces, and another ten months before she was even put together.

        1. The Statue was a gift from the French to the Americans, however the Americans were to supply the pedestal for the statue.

            a. The wait to put her up came from the Americans not having a pedestal to put the statue on, due to lack of money.

            b. According to authors Bell and Abrams of In Search of Liberty, people had the following attitudes:

1) Some Americans said the French should pay for the pedestal.

2) Others thought it was a disgrace to have a splendid gift without providing a landing place for it.

c. Meanwhile, Congress voted using Treasury funds for the pedestal.

2. Joseph Pulitzer, Editor of "The World," newspaper, said he would publish everyone's name who contributed a penny or more to the fund for the pedestal.

a. According to Statue Of Liberty video sponsored by PBS, most of the people who contributed were, low income, children and immigrants.

b. And, in just a few weeks, "The World" had more than $100,000 which was almost all donated in a dollar or less.

CONCLUSION

The Statue of Liberty finally stood tall 21 years after the idea that the French would give the Americans a statue. I hope that each one of you in your future, when you see the Statue of Liberty will remember how it represents our freedom and that you remember the history: who and how the idea to build a statue for America, the design of the statue, and how the statue traveled over seas and had to wait for a pedestal. I would like to close with a quote from Thomas Jefferson, "We hold these truths to be self-evident, that all men are created equal, that they are endowed by their Creator with certain unalienable Rights, that among these are Life, Liberty, and the pursuit of Happiness."

BIBLIOGRAPHY

Bell, J.B. and Abrams, R.I. In Search of Liberty. New York. 1984.

Dillon, W.S. and Kotler, N.G. The Statue of Liberty Revisited. 1994.

Compton's Interactive Encyclopedia. 1997.

Handlin, O. "Statue of Liberty." Newsweek. New York.

VIDEO TAPES

_____. A&E. The Statue of Liberty Video tape.

PBS. Ken Burn's America Collection--Statue of Liberty.

_____. "Statue of Liberty, National Monument and Ellis Island." The National Park Service.

VISUAL AIDS

Four Overheads: Laboulaye, Bartholdi, Frame of "Statue of Liberty", and "The World" Newspaper.

"PROFILE OF THE SERIAL KILLER"

By Ken Brower
(Reprinted with permission.)

INTRODUCTION

"I hated all of my life. I hated everybody. When I first grew up, I was dressed as a girl by my Mother. ...And after that I was treated like what I call the dog of the family. I was beaten; I was made to do things that no human being would want to do... Then I started to do anything I could do to get away from home... but I couldn't get away from it. I even went to Michigan... my mother came up there and we got into an argument in a beer tavern. That's when I killed her."

The quote is from Henry Lee Lucas, currently on death row in Texas for eleven murder convictions. Badly abused as a youngster, he claims that he committed his first murder at the age of fifteen.

The FBI estimates that there are at least 35 serial killers on the loose and under investigation in the United States. Killers like Ted Bundy and Jeffrey Dahmer. What caused these monsters to commit unspeakable acts torture and murder? Through examining their common characteristics and motivations for killing we will try to peek into the mind of the serial killer.

THESIS

Serial killers may be understood by examining their common characteristics, childhood trauma, and motives for killing.

BODY

I. Serial killers may be defined using a common set of characteristics.
   A. According to David Lester, PhD, a serial killer can be defined as someone who kills three or more people with a "cooling off period" (typically 30 days) between killings.
      1. This is not to be confused with a mass murderer.
      2. That would be like Timothy McVeigh, who kills many people at one time without the cooling off period.
   B. He is male, between the ages of 25-35, and white.
   C. The majority of the time, he will kill white victims.
   D. He will typically keep killing until forced to stop.
   E. Unlike typical murders in the news, his victims are typically strangers.
   F. Researcher Dr. Vernon Mark, retired chief of neurosurgery at Boston General Hospital, has demonstrated that frontal lobe damage was common amongst serial killers.
      1. Damage to the temporal lobe can cause confusion and bewilderment for hours or even days, and may also cause hair trigger violent reactions against persons perceived as threats.
      2. Robert Long, who killed 10 people in Florida in 1984, suffered from numerous blows to the head.
         a. As a child, he fell from a swing and had his eye pierced by a stick.
         b. The year after that he was hit by a car and had a severe concussion.
         c. A few years later he was involved in a motorcycle crash that fractured his skull.

(TRANSITION: In addition to these common characteristics...)

II. Researchers identify childhood trauma as potential causes of their behavior.
   A. An FBI report also lists several childhood problems that occurred with alarming frequency amongst serial killers.
      1. Many had shown cruelty to animals and other neighborhood children.
      2. Daydreaming and fantasizing was common.
      3. Most played alone or were forced to spend hours alone.
      4. Almost all were pathological liars.
      5. Many experienced bed wetting beyond age 6 or 7.
   B. Henry Lee Lucas experienced a traumatic young life.
      1. His father killed himself after repeatedly being humiliated by his abusive prostitute wife.
      2. When Henry cut his eye while playing with a knife his mother left his gashed eye unattended for days until it eventually withered and had to be removed by a doctor.
      3. Once his mom beat him so severely with a piece of wood that he lay in a semi-conscious state for three days before her boyfriend decided to take him to a local hospital.
      4. Another time, she cruelly decided to send him to school in a dress and with his hair curled.

(TRANSITION: As we can see, serial killers share startling common factors that contribute to their violent tendencies. Next, we'll try to get into the mind of the serial murderer to examine their motives for killing.)

III. According to Joel Norris in Serial Killers, serial killers have three basic motives: visionary, missionary, and lust which drives their passion for murder.
   A. The Visionary Motive Type is the group considered insane or psychotic, often hearing voices in their head that tell them to commit the crime.
      1. David Berkowitz's, known as the Son of Sam, regarding his neighbors possessed dog, said:
      2. "He won't let me stop killing until he gets his fill of blood."
   B. The Missionary-Oriented killer tries to rid the world of a category of people he considers unworthy.
      1. Ted Kaczinsky, the Unabomber, targeted university professors in the mathematics and science fields in his battle against technology.
      2. "All the university people whom we have attacked have been specialists in technical fields. ...The people we are out to get are the scientists and engineers, especially in critical fields like computers and genetics." (Letter from the Unabomber to the NY Times.)
   C. The Lust Killer, the most common type of serial murderer, kills for the pure turn on, yet they are in touch with reality and may have relationships.
      1. [Story of Carol DaRonch] While at the mall, a handsome, well-dressed man approached 18-year-old Carol DaRonch. He told her that someone had tried to break into her car, and she needed to come take a look. He had an authoritative air that made her assume he was a security guard or officer. She followed him quietly out of the building to her car. Even though there was nothing missing, he told her she needed to come to the station to see if she knew the suspect. It wasn't until they were in his Volkswagen that she smelled alcohol on his breath. When he told her to put on her seat belt, she said no, and was ready to jump, but he'd already started driving and was going very fast. She realized he was heading away from the police station. Suddenly he screeched to a halt and tried to handcuffed her, but in the struggle, connected both cuffs to the same wrist. As they struggled, he pulled out a small gun and threatened her with it. She fell out of the car, and as she got up, he came at her with a crowbar. He threw her up against the car, and in a sheer adrenaline rush brought on by utter terror, Carol DaRonch broke free from her attacker and ran wildly to the road. An older couple came upon her just in time and took the terrified girl to the police station. She was their first living, breathing victim of serial killer Ted Bundy.

162

2. Ted Bundy, believed to have killed over 36 women, is one of America's most famous lust serial killers.

CONCLUSION

According to Dorothy Lewis, MD, renowned for her study of serial killers, theorized that "given certain kinds of neurological and psychiatric problems, and being raised by violent, abusive parents, just about any of us could be turned into a killer... We now know that intense, ongoing emotional stress can change the very structure of our brain. No one is immune. It could happen to any of us."

By studying the childhood trauma, frequency of severe brain injury, and the four motives for killing, we took a peek into the hideous minds of these serial killers. Maybe one day doctors will be able to isolate and remove these monsters from society before they destroy peoples' lives. Until then, we can only hope that we don't unknowingly cross paths with that of the serial killer.

BIBLIOGRAPHY

Lewis, Dorothy Otnow, M.D. Guilty By Reason of Insanity. New York: Random House. 1998.

Lester, David, PhD. Serial Killers: The Insatiable Passion. Philadelphia, PA: Charles Press Publishers. 1995.

Norris, Joel. Serial Killers. New York: Anchor Books. 1998.

VISUAL AIDS

Famous serial killers - overhead transparency
Common characteristics - overhead transparency
Childhood warning signs - overhead transparency
Motives for killing - overhead transparency

"TAKING CARE OF MAN'S BEST FRIEND"

By Lisa Golden
(Reprinted with permission.)

INTRODUCTION

Often is the case that people think of puppies as being so cute and adorable that they just have to get one. This is all fine and well, but the people forget to think about the responsibility that comes with the beloved dog. So is the case with the Smiths.

Mr. and Mrs. Smith, a couple I have invented for the speech, both thought a dog would be so cute to have. Mr. Smith imagined running on the beach with Fido and playing Frisbee with him, and Mrs. Smith thought about hugging the precious little puppy. They both agreed on adopting a puppy for themselves, and since both Mr. and Mrs. Smith work, they thought it would be convenient to have a Dalmatian puppy delivered to their home, via airmail express.

Apple, a ten-week-old pup arrived at the Smiths' home scared to death. She would not move out of her crate for hours and would not eat for days. As Apple grew older, she never could shake her puppy hood experience, and because the Smiths never had the time to work with her she was afraid of people, didn't like to be held, and was afraid whenever she was outside the house. This was not the dog that the Smiths had envisioned, nor was this the treatment that Apple deserved. The Smiths could have avoided this situation if they would have prepared themselves better for a dog.

So this never has to happen to anybody here, I would like to take this opportunity to inform you about how to avoid this disaster. I have been a dog owner for several years and have learned many useful ways to make pet ownership a good experience. Even if you aren't thinking about adopting a dog today, there's a good chance that one day the thought might cross your mind, and you will have been prepared.

THESIS

Successfully adopting a puppy requires that you understand three key elements: first, deciding if a dog is the right choice for you; second, preparing for your pup's arrival; and third, knowing the basic care for your new puppy.

(TRANSITION: Now for the first of the three key elements.)

BODY

I. Before obtaining a dog, you should first decide if a dog is the right pet for you, by considering a few basic facts about dogs and asking yourself some important questions.

   A. A few basic facts to know about dogs, from Good Housekeeping's Guide to Dogs and Training, are listed as follows.

      1. A dog should live to be over a decade old, so you should plan on caring for the dog for this long.

      2. Dogs are solely dependent on their people to be fed, groomed, exercised, and taken to the vet.

      3. It costs money to adopt and care for a dog.

B. Not only is it an essential to know some facts about dogs before you decide to get one, but it is also a good idea to ask yourself some questions like these that come from, <u>Good Owners, Great Dogs</u>, by Brian Kilcommons.

  1. Do I have enough time to spend with my dog each day?

  2. Do I live in a city apartment or do I have a fifty-acre farm in the country?

  3. Does a dog fit my lifestyle?

(TRANSITION: After reviewing the facts about dogs and answering some questions about dogs, then you are ready to move to the next step of the process, which is the preparation for your puppy.)

II. According to <u>The Complete Dog Care Manual</u>, by Bruce Fogle, D.V.M., and <u>Good Owners, Great Dogs</u> there are three important things to do when preparing for your new pup: first, decide where you will get your pup; second, know what to look for in a pup; and, third, you must prepare your home for the new pup.

  A. There are two good places you can get your new pup from; either a reputable breeder, or a shelter.

    1. If you are looking for a pure breed, then a breeder is the best place to look.

    2. If the breed doesn't matter to you, then shelters are a wonderful source of pets who desperately need homes.

  B. In Kilcommons book, he gives a list of four tests to look for good temperament in a puppy.

    1. The Cradle Test where you pick up a puppy, cradle it, and see what its response is, tests for a relaxed puppy in tense situations.

    2. The Touch-Sensitivity Test, where you squeeze the webbing between the pup's toes and see if the pup responds to the pressure, tests his pain tolerance.

    3. The Sound-Sensitivity Test, where you would drop a ring of keys next to the puppy and see if he reacts, tests to see if the pup can cope with noise in a positive way.

    4. The Attraction Test, where you set the pup down some feet away from you, then see if the pup is interested and comes over to you, tests to see if the pup is people oriented.

  C. According to <u>The Complete Dog Care Manual</u>, you must have a few important items in the house before you bring your pup home.

    1. You must select a crate for your dog, where he can feel safe and secure.

    2. Puppies also need food dishes and fresh water made available to them at all times.

    3. You should also be ready to invest in a lot of newspaper for accidents your puppy might have.

(TRANSITION: After carefully selecting a puppy, and getting your home ready for the puppy, you should be aware of the basic health care your new puppy requires.)

III. A few important guidelines to follow on caring for your new pup come from <u>Good Owners, Great Dogs</u>, and have to do with your puppy's health in the first year of its life.

   A. Make your first veterinarian appointment within two days of bringing your puppy home.

      1. Bring with you your puppy's health record, if you have one, a stool sample, and your puppy on a leash and collar.

      2. Your puppy's first visit to the vet will include an examination, vaccinations, and a parasite check.

   B. The single most important thing you could ever do for your puppy is to get it spayed or neutered.

      1. After the age of six months is a good time to get your puppy fixed.

      2. With 13 million dogs being killed because of overpopulation, there is no excuse for not getting your dog spayed or neutered.

(TRANSITION: These last guidelines are vital to the care of your puppy)

CONCLUSION

    In conclusion, if you follow my three key elements, which are deciding if a dog is the right pet for you, preparing for your puppy's arrival, and following the basic guidelines for your puppy's care, then you will be quite successful in adopting a puppy the right way.

    It is important for you to know how to plan for the adoption of a puppy so you can be prepared if the time ever comes about, and not end up like the Smiths.

    The poor Smiths. If they only would have thought more sensibly about the reasons why they wanted a dog, by knowing some facts about dogs, and asking themselves some questions about how they would care for a dog, they probably would have been able to see that they didn't have the time to care for a dog, and would have avoided the pain they went through with Apple.

    In any event, if you or someone you know is thinking about getting a puppy, tell them to plan carefully, be prepared, and care for the puppy correctly, because like the title of Brian Kilcommons' book says, "Great Owners Make Great Dogs."

BIBLIOGRAPHY

Fogle, B., D.V.M. <u>Complete Dog Care Manual</u>. New York: Dorling Kindersley Inc. 1993

Kilcommons, B. <u>Good Owners, Great Dogs</u>. New York: Warner Books Inc. 1992

Wolforth, M. G. <u>Good Housekeeping Guide to Dog Care and Training</u>. New York: Hearst Co. 1977.

VISUAL AIDS

    Large color pictures of puppies
    Overhead: "Guidelines" from <u>Good Owners, Great Dogs</u>

ASSIGNMENT: Peer Editing of Speech Outline

SPEAKER_____ PEER EDITOR_____

INSTRUCTIONS: As the speaker delivers the speech from manuscript, check the following:

1) From the list on page 149 circle the type(s) of Attention Device(s) you heard in the introduction.
    Rhetorical Questions, Illustration/Anecdotes, Startling Statement, Quotation, Humor, Action, None,
    Other (explain):

2) What did the speaker say in the credibility statement?

3) Write out the thesis PURPOSE

    and thesis PREVIEW

4) Count and list the sources cited during the speech.

    NONE
    1.
    2.
    3.
    4.

5) Using page 134, identify 3 to 5 types of supporting information used in the speech and write a few
    words to indicate how they are used.
    1.

    2.

    3.

    4.

    5.

6) WHERE are the audio/visual aids used in the speech? WHEN are they used?

7) What is the summary of the main points to begin the conclusion?

8) From the list on page 149 circle the type(s) of Clincher(s) you heard in the conclusion.
    Rhetorical Questions, Illustration/Anecdotes, Startling Statement, Quotation, Humor, Action, None,
    Other (explain):

9) What questions could you ask of the speaker to begin the "question period" after the speech?

Cover Sheet: Informative Speech Outline

INFORMATIVE SPEECH EVALUATION (INSTRUCTOR EVALUATION)

STUDENT SPEAKER_____

THE SPEECH ITSELF
    INTRODUCTION   (9)_____
        Attention Device
        Credibility Statement
    THESIS   (5)_____
        Thesis Purpose
        Thesis Preview
    BODY
        CLEAR MAIN POINTS/ORGANIZATION   (10)_____
        Easy to Identify
        Appropriate Emphasis
        Organization Clear
        Mutually Exclusive
        Connectives/Transitions
        SUPPORTING INFORMATION   (20)_____
        Concrete Examples
        Concrete Evidence
        Appropriate Sources
        CITATIONS OF 3 SOURCES   (6)_____

    CONCLUSION   (9)_____
        Summary of Main Points
        Audience Closure
        Clincher
    VISUAL/AUDIO AIDS   (5)_____

    DELIVERY   (20)_____
        Extemporaneous
        Natural
        Good use of Eye Contact
        No Distracting Movement or Sounds
        Appropriate Voice Volume
        Appropriate Voice Variety (not a monotone)
        Appropriate Speaking Rate
    OVERALL EFFECT   (6)_____

                                      TOTAL: (90)_____

STRENGTHS

SUGGESTED CHANGES TO MAKE BEFORE YOUR FINAL SPEECH

Critique Form: **Informative Speech**

SPEAKER_____

TOPIC_____

INSTRUCTIONS: Rate the speaker on each of the first 12 categories by circling the term which best describes this element of the speech. Complete the second portion of the evaluation by making specific comments which respond to the phrases. Be as helpful as possible as all speakers can benefit from constructive feedback.

INTRODUCTION

Attention Device   Excellent Good Average Fair Weak Missing

Credibility Statement   Excellent Good Average Fair Weak Missing

THESIS

Clear Purpose   Excellent Good Average Fair Weak Missing

Clear Preview   Excellent Good Average Fair Weak Missing

BODY

Main Points Clear   Excellent Good Average Fair Weak Missing

Quantity of Support Information   Excellent Good Average Fair Weak Missing

Quality of Support Information   Excellent Good Average Fair Weak Missing

CONCLUSION

Summary Clear   Excellent Good Average Fair Weak Missing

Audience Closure/Clincher   Excellent Good Average Fair Weak Missing

DELIVERY

Eye Contact   Excellent Good Average Fair Weak Missing

Gestures   Excellent Good Average Fair Weak Missing

Use of Voice   Excellent Good Average Fair Weak Missing

The single best thing about this speech was:

If the speaker had made this change his/her speech would have been considerably improved:

Critic_____

(YOUR NAME WILL BE REMOVED)

171

Critique Form: **Informative Speech**

SPEAKER_____

TOPIC_____

INSTRUCTIONS: Rate the speaker on each of the first 12 categories by circling the term which best describes this element of the speech. Complete the second portion of the evaluation by making specific comments which respond to the phrases. Be as helpful as possible as all speakers can benefit from constructive feedback.

INTRODUCTION

Attention Device   Excellent Good Average Fair Weak Missing

Credibility Statement   Excellent Good Average Fair Weak Missing

THESIS

Clear Purpose   Excellent Good Average Fair Weak Missing

Clear Preview   Excellent Good Average Fair Weak Missing

BODY

Main Points Clear   Excellent Good Average Fair Weak Missing

Quantity of Support Information   Excellent Good Average Fair Weak Missing

Quality of Support Information   Excellent Good Average Fair Weak Missing

CONCLUSION

Summary Clear   Excellent Good Average Fair Weak Missing

Audience Closure/Clincher   Excellent Good Average Fair Weak Missing

DELIVERY

Eye Contact   Excellent Good Average Fair Weak Missing

Gestures   Excellent Good Average Fair Weak Missing

Use of Voice   Excellent Good Average Fair Weak Missing

The single best thing about this speech was:

If the speaker had made this change his/her speech would have been considerably improved:

Critic_____
(YOUR NAME WILL BE REMOVED)

Critique Form: **Informative Speech**

SPEAKER_____

TOPIC_____

INSTRUCTIONS: Rate the speaker on each of the first 12 categories by circling the term which best describes this element of the speech. Complete the second portion of the evaluation by making specific comments which respond to the phrases. Be as helpful as possible as all speakers can benefit from constructive feedback.

INTRODUCTION

Attention Device   Excellent Good Average Fair Weak Missing

Credibility Statement   Excellent Good Average Fair Weak Missing

THESIS

Clear Purpose   Excellent Good Average Fair Weak Missing

Clear Preview   Excellent Good Average Fair Weak Missing

BODY

Main Points Clear   Excellent Good Average Fair Weak Missing

Quantity of Support Information   Excellent Good Average Fair Weak Missing

Quality of Support Information   Excellent Good Average Fair Weak Missing

CONCLUSION

Summary Clear   Excellent Good Average Fair Weak Missing

Audience Closure/Clincher   Excellent Good Average Fair Weak Missing

DELIVERY

Eye Contact   Excellent Good Average Fair Weak Missing

Gestures   Excellent Good Average Fair Weak Missing

Use of Voice   Excellent Good Average Fair Weak Missing

The single best thing about this speech was:

If the speaker had made this change his/her speech would have been considerably improved:

Critic_____

(YOUR NAME WILL BE REMOVED)

175

Critique Form: **Informative Speech**

SPEAKER_____

TOPIC_____

INSTRUCTIONS: Rate the speaker on each of the first 12 categories by circling the term which best describes this element of the speech. Complete the second portion of the evaluation by making specific comments which respond to the phrases. Be as helpful as possible as all speakers can benefit from constructive feedback.

INTRODUCTION

Attention Device   Excellent Good Average Fair Weak Missing

Credibility Statement   Excellent Good Average Fair Weak Missing

THESIS

Clear Purpose   Excellent Good Average Fair Weak Missing

Clear Preview   Excellent Good Average Fair Weak Missing

BODY

Main Points Clear   Excellent Good Average Fair Weak Missing

Quantity of Support Information   Excellent Good Average Fair Weak Missing

Quality of Support Information   Excellent Good Average Fair Weak Missing

CONCLUSION

Summary Clear   Excellent Good Average Fair Weak Missing

Audience Closure/Clincher Excellent Good Average Fair Weak Missing

DELIVERY

Eye Contact   Excellent Good Average Fair Weak Missing

Gestures   Excellent Good Average Fair Weak Missing

Use of Voice   Excellent Good Average Fair Weak Missing

The single best thing about this speech was:

If the speaker had made this change his/her speech would have been considerably improved:

Critic_____

(YOUR NAME WILL BE REMOVED)

Critique Form: **Informative Speech**

SPEAKER_____

TOPIC_____

INSTRUCTIONS: Rate the speaker on each of the first 12 categories by circling the term which best describes this element of the speech. Complete the second portion of the evaluation by making specific comments which respond to the phrases. Be as helpful as possible as all speakers can benefit from constructive feedback.

INTRODUCTION

Attention Device   Excellent Good Average Fair Weak Missing

Credibility Statement   Excellent Good Average Fair Weak Missing

THESIS

Clear Purpose   Excellent Good Average Fair Weak Missing

Clear Preview   Excellent Good Average Fair Weak Missing

BODY

Main Points Clear   Excellent Good Average Fair Weak Missing

Quantity of Support Information   Excellent Good Average Fair Weak Missing

Quality of Support Information   Excellent Good Average Fair Weak Missing

CONCLUSION

Summary Clear   Excellent Good Average Fair Weak Missing

Audience Closure/Clincher   Excellent Good Average Fair Weak Missing

DELIVERY

Eye Contact   Excellent Good Average Fair Weak Missing

Gestures   Excellent Good Average Fair Weak Missing

Use of Voice   Excellent Good Average Fair Weak Missing

The single best thing about this speech was:

If the speaker had made this change his/her speech would have been considerably improved:

Critic_____
(YOUR NAME WILL BE REMOVED)

Critique Form: **Informative Speech**

SPEAKER_____

TOPIC_____

INSTRUCTIONS: Rate the speaker on each of the first 12 categories by circling the term which best describes this element of the speech. Complete the second portion of the evaluation by making specific comments which respond to the phrases. Be as helpful as possible as all speakers can benefit from constructive feedback.

INTRODUCTION

Attention Device   Excellent Good Average Fair Weak Missing

Credibility Statement   Excellent Good Average Fair Weak Missing

THESIS

Clear Purpose   Excellent Good Average Fair Weak Missing

Clear Preview   Excellent Good Average Fair Weak Missing

BODY

Main Points Clear   Excellent Good Average Fair Weak Missing

Quantity of Support Information   Excellent Good Average Fair Weak Missing

Quality of Support Information   Excellent Good Average Fair Weak Missing

CONCLUSION

Summary Clear   Excellent Good Average Fair Weak Missing

Audience Closure/Clincher   Excellent Good Average Fair Weak Missing

DELIVERY

Eye Contact   Excellent Good Average Fair Weak Missing

Gestures   Excellent Good Average Fair Weak Missing

Use of Voice   Excellent Good Average Fair Weak Missing

The single best thing about this speech was:

If the speaker had made this change his/her speech would have been considerably improved:

Critic_____

(YOUR NAME WILL BE REMOVED)

DUE ONE WEEK AFTER SPEECH DELIVERY:

ASSIGNMENT: Personal Evaluation of Informative Speech

COMPLETE THIS FORM AFTER YOU VIEW THE VIDEO TAPE OF YOUR SPEECH

NAME_____

SPEECH TITLE_____

1. What was the specific purpose of your speech?

   How well do you feel you achieved that purpose?

2. Comment about each of the four parts of the speech.

   INTRODUCTION

   THESIS

   BODY AND SUPPORTING INFORMATION

   CONCLUSION

3. How comfortable and confident did you feel during the speech?

   Does the video tape show you as more or less comfortable and confident than you really were?

4. SPEECH CONTENT
   What is one point in the content you are proud of from this speech?

   What is one point about the content you would change if you could do the speech again?

5. DELIVERY
   What points about your delivery please you as you view the tape?

   What points in delivery will you work on before you give the next speech to the class?

6. Were you as prepared for the speech as you wanted to be?

THE SPEECH TO PERSUADE

Assignment Specifics

PURPOSE:

1. In this speech your purpose is to design a desired persuasive outcome for your speech based on your knowledge of this audience and your specific audience analysis. You will build an "argument" which is called a *persuasive strategy* for your point of view and present it to the audience. You will tailor-make the speech to fit your skills and strengths as a speaker and to match the specific nature of your audience.

2. Your goal is to change your audience -- change their attitudes or behaviors.

REQUIREMENTS:

1. A 6 to 8 minute speech which will be timed and penalized if over or under the required time limit

2. Must somehow link to informative speech

3. Must consider Audience Analysis

4. Speaker may take only note cards and audio/visual aids to the front of the room

5. Extemporaneous Style (planned, practiced, and seemingly spontaneous)

6. Visual Aids may be used

7. At least 3 sources of information cited in Bibliography -- with citations in speech only for those used directly in the speech

8. Working outlines presented to Support Group prior to speech

9. Full sentence outline and Bibliography due on day speech is presented to class

10. Speaker will be introduced by a member of the Support Group

11. The speech should reflect your attention to the three persuasive proofs that are from Aristotle's theory of rhetoric.

12. Videotape -- Speaker provides a personal videotape to the camera operator prior to the speech.

Workshop Activity: **Linking the Speech to Inform and the Speech to Persuade**

Example: The Speech to Inform and the Speech to Persuade have a direct link in the following example.

SPEECH #1   Topic: Organ Transplants
            General Purpose: To Inform
            Specific Purpose: After listening to my speech the audience will be able to list three uncommon types of organ transplants.
            Thesis Statement: Transplants now can replace a great variety of organs such as the retina, bone marrow, and the liver.

SPEECH #2   Topic: How to become an Organ Donor
            General Purpose: To Persuade
            Specific Purpose: After listening to my speech 75% of the members of my audience will either affirm that they carry signed donor cards or will sign the donor card I will have given them during the speech.
            Proposition: Any one of us can contribute to medical science and future generations by simply signing our name.

In this example, the connection between the two speeches is less predictable -- and maybe you can surprise us with the position you take for your persuasive speech. Consider the following Informative Speech Plan:

SPEECH #1   Topic: Freedom
            General Purpose: To Inform
            Specific Purpose: After listening to my speech the audience will understand my definition of freedom and why freedom is so important to me.
            Thesis Statement: Freedom can be defined personally, by your family, and by your future goals.

Please write out your idea for the plan for the Persuasive Speech. We will share these in class.

SPEECH #2   Topic:

            General Purpose:

            Specific Purpose:

            Proposition:

            Main Points:

Three Persuasive Proofs: Logos, Pathos, Ethos

The words Logos, Pathos, and Ethos are classic Greek terms that simply recognize the fact that when we attempt to "persuade" people to change their attitudes or behavior, we must approach the task in more than one way in order to achieve some success.

The term Logos refers to the dimension of a persuasive speech that rests on rational, objectively verifiable, logical proof. (The word logic comes from the Greek word *logos*, which means, essentially, "reason," or "rational thought and expression.") And, of course, to persuade rational people, you must provide them with the examples, statistics, quotes from authorities, scientific data, historical references, news events, etc., without which your argument will seem thin and just plain unconvincing, no matter how much you may care about it.

But, human beings are not disembodied intellects, computers with arms and legs. We are emotional; we have strong feelings for things we care about. The term Pathos refers to this passionate, "feeling" dimension to the persuasive speech. It is the emotional "hook" which gets people to pay attention to your objective, rational, logical argument. It is what draws people in. (Consider that words such as sympathy or empathy are derived from the original Greek word *pathos*.) To start with, you should be emotionally involved with your speech topic if you want to persuade others to care about it. You should speak about a subject you find important, or beautiful, or urgent, perhaps because it has touched your life in a way that matters. Your own emotional involvement will be communicated to the audience. Remember, however, that Pathos must be balanced with Logos. Reason without emotion is cold and distant; but emotion without rational, objective substantiation is manipulative, and the audience will resent it.

Ethos is most commonly translated to mean credibility. When Aristotle spoke about ethos he defined it as intelligence, character and goodwill. In modern times we think of ethos as dynamism, appearance, and honesty. It has to do with the way you "connect" with your audience, so that they respect what you have to say. If they believe in you as a person, they won't close their minds to your "proposition." (Consider the related word "ethical.") We are best persuaded by people we respect. Just as with good interpersonal communication, so too with public speaking, the principle of **mutuality** applies: We tend to respect those who respect us. Respect goes both ways. How does a speaker win the positive regard of his or her audience? Here are some suggestions:

In summary, logos shows that you have carefully researched the topic, cited your sources correctly, and your message is well organized and reasonable. Pathos can be seen in the passion in your delivery, through the language you use including imagery and metaphor, and through the forms of supporting information you use to clarify your main points. Ethos begins with your statement of credibility and includes dynamism, your knowledge of your subject and audience, and through the credibility of the sources you cite in the speech.

The bottom line is to prepare well. If the audience sees that you respected them and your subject enough to put a lot of work into preparing and practicing your speech, they will respect you in return, even if they don't share your point of view.

Don't try to "browbeat" or "shock" your audience into agreeing with you. That never works. It doesn't work because the audience will resent such an aggressive approach. Wouldn't you? (For this reason, there are some "loaded" issues which are, perhaps, not suitable for an eight-minute speech.) Consider an obvious, but often overlooked, fact: It is those who don't agree with your proposition that you are trying to persuade. Be sure that you don't choose a subject about which you are close-minded, or you will fall into the "shock" and "browbeat" mode, and your target audience will be annoyed, but not persuaded.

Here's a related idea: Don't ignore your opponent's point of view. You gain the respect of your audience by acknowledging your opponent's arguments and then refuting them-- logically, concretely, and respectfully. (This can also be a useful organizing principle.)

You might acknowledge your audience, perhaps referring to a previous speech that relates to your topic, or possibly using the results of your Audience Analysis. The audience will respect the fact that you take them seriously.

If the topic you have chosen touches you personally, the audience will respect your allowing them to know this, if that is appropriate to your purpose. Perhaps some brief anecdotal material can be used in developing your proposition.

ASSIGNMENT: Audience Analysis

After you have presented your informative speech you will have the opportunity to gather some information from the members of the class (prospective audience) which will help you prepare for the persuasive speech. On an assigned date each student will distribute an Audience Analysis Survey to every other member of the class.

You should design your audience analysis in such a way that it gives you information you need to help you know how to approach the audience with your persuasive argument. As you write your audience analysis keep asking yourself: "What do I need to know about these audience members that will help me persuade them to my point of view?"

An audience analysis contains only **OBJECTIVE QUESTIONS**. We do not have the time to write down our views for you. We need to be able to answer "yes" or "no" to a question, or to circle a response, or to write just one word to answer your questions. These are some examples you may consider.

DEMOGRAPHIC INFORMATION: Age, Sex, Family Size, Political Party, Married or Single. (Written in question or multiple-choice form.)

"YES" or "NO" ANSWERS: (Written in simple questions.)

Example: Do you own a car? Yes or No

LIKERT SCALE STATEMENTS: (Written in Declarative Sentences)

Example:

The speed limit on highways should be 75 mph.
DISAGREE 1 2 3 4 5 6 7 AGREE

STATE YOUR PROPOSITION (THESIS): You want to know the audience opinion of your general position. (Written in the form of a Proposition of Value or a Proposition of Policy)

Examples: Proposition of VALUE

Bill Clinton was a good president.
DISAGREE 1 2 3 4 5 6 7 AGREE

It is a privilege to serve a term of jury duty.
DISAGREE 1 2 3 4 5 6 7 AGREE

Examples: Proposition of POLICY

The federal government should legalize marijuana for private use.
DISAGREE 1 2 3 4 5 6 7 AGREE

Abortion should remain legal in the United States.
DISAGREE 1 2 3 4 5 6 7 AGREE

NOTE: On "Audience Analysis Day" you will need to have the proper number of copies of your survey to distribute to the class.

ITEMS: Your Audience Analysis Survey can contain up to 10 items.

(Example of Audience Analysis Survey follows on next page.)

Example: **Audience Analysis Survey**

Audience Analysis Survey

By Jennifer Mickwee
(Reprinted with permission.)

1. Do you currently pay income tax?   ___yes   ___no

2. Approximately what is your annual income?
    under $25,000___ $25,000-50,000___   above $50,000___

3. Are you: ___a republican   or   ___a democrat   or   ___other

4. Are you happy with the current income tax system?   ___yes   ___no

5. If you are not happy, why? (you can check more than one)
    ___too complex
    ___unfair
    ___too many loopholes
    ___double taxation
    ___other (please specify)_____

6. On a scale of 1 - 9, how familiar are you with the proposed Flat Tax, or Flat Rate System?
    (Please circle one)

    1   2   3   4   5   6   7   8   9
    unfamiliar   familiar

7. Do you believe adopting a flat rate of 19% for every taxpayer would be more or less beneficial than
    keeping the current income tax system?
    ___More beneficial   ___Undecided   ___Less Beneficial

8. If you checked "Less Beneficial," Why?
    ___unfair
    ___doesn't create enough revenue
    ___takes away incentive to donate to charity
    ___other (please specify)_____

9. Are you taxed twice because you hold stock in a corporation?
    ___yes   ___no

10. If you are currently giving to charity, would you continue to give if you did not get a tax break?
    ___yes   ___no   ___I don't give to charity

Examples: **Full Sentence Outlines for Speeches to Persuade**

"THE CRY FOR HELP"

By Lisa Golden
(Reprinted with permission.)

INTRODUCTION

Have you ever bought something from a store, brought it home, tried it on again, only to decide you didn't like it? Sure, we all have at one time or another, so we try to take it back to the store to get a refund and find out it is the store's policy that we can't. So, we try to do the next best thing, exchange the item for something we do want.

The hypothetical Smith family, from my informative speech, couldn't return their dog Apple, so Mr. Smith, being business minded, thought it would be wise to try to exchange Apple for something the family would like and in doing so added a costly price to Apple's welfare. Since Apple was a purebred Dalmatian, Mr. Smith thought he would breed her and get a pup from the litter that the family would approve of.

Just as luck would have it the Smith's neighbors had a purebred Dalmatian and agreed to breed Apple with their dog. Apple soon was impregnated and had a litter of nine pups. All of the nine pups were born deaf as a result of genetic over breeding in the Dalmatian breed, which will commonly show up when these dogs are bred together. The neighbor didn't want any of the deaf pups and neither did Mr. Smith. He didn't want to keep Apple either, so Apple and her litter of nine were taken to the local pound, to have a maximum limit of two weeks to be adopted before they would die.

There is no reason for the senseless breeding of animals when there are already too many animals in the country to take care of. In the survey I took in our class on March the third, 22 out of 26 people said that they cared a lot about the welfare of animals. So today, I would like to take this opportunity to alert those who care, and even those who do not care, since the problem involves everyone, about the animal crisis, and the only solution that we must act on to prevent the crisis.

PROPOSITION

In order to overcome some of the harsh realities of pet overpopulation, we must adopt a new and improved solution.

(TRANSITION: Let me first start with the shocking truth of the problem.)

BODY

I. Pet overpopulation is a serious problem that is not being handled properly in our society.

   A. The animal overpopulation problem is simply defined as the fact that there are too many cats and dogs and too few homes for them.

      1. According to the "Fund for Animals Fact Sheet," out of the 27 million cats and dogs born each year, 10 to 13 million we classify as "surplus," and kill.

      2. Most of these animals are young and healthy; in fact, it is estimated that the majority we kill are less than one year of age.

B. The solution that our society has adopted for the problem is to kill the "surplus," or extras.

   1. This solution has been considered acceptable without fault as though there were no other way to control the crisis.

   2. Yet, we spend over 1 billion dollars every year destroying "man's best friend."

C. The cause of the problem is irresponsible guardians.

   1. By irresponsible guardians I mean all people who don't spay or neuter their dog or cat.

   2. This is why it is important to be informed on how to prepare and care for your pet before you adopt, so we can prevent overpopulation.

(TRANSITION: After hearing these facts, we are now ready to appreciate the credibility of my solution to the problem.)

II. Because of the failing solutions already in effect, the only solution to the overpopulation problem with ethical, financial, and health and safety advantages would be for each of us to take the personal responsibility to spay/neuter our pets.

A. It is necessary to take personal responsibility to spay/neuter pets because other efforts currently made to control the problem are not working.

   1. Killing the extras is not solving the overpopulation problem; it is merely controlling it temporarily in an unethical way and at a great financial cost to our communities.

   2. Although humane education programs and low cost spay/neuter clinics are good efforts, they are still not effective enough to control the problem.

B. Some advantages to taking personal responsibility to spay/neuter pets, from the "Euthanasia is a Euphemism" Pamphlet, put out by The Fund for Animals based in Vacaville, CA. include, ethical, financial, and health and safety advantages.

   1. Reducing the number of animals born is the only ethical solution to the over population problem with long-term effects rather than killing the extras.

   2. It would cost less to prevent animals from being born each year than the one billion dollars we spend killing the extras each year.

   3. Reducing the number of animals born will have an impact on public health and safety by reducing the number of dog bites, animals causing traffic hazards, dogs running loose, quarantines, and everyone's "pet" peeve, dog droppings.

(TRANSITION: Now that we know why it is important for animal owners to take personal responsibility, let's see what else we can do.)

III. Some other ways of trying to help curb the problem are as follows.

A. If you have enough time you can help set up a Breeding Ban Ordinance in your community.

1. You can do this by checking with your local animal shelter to see if they have a program started that you can join.
2. If your community does not already have such a program, you can start one by writing for more information to: The Fund for Animals, 808 Alamo Dr., Suite 306, Vacaville, CA. 95688.

B. If you don't have enough time on your hands to set up a Breeding Ban Ordinance, then you can do things on more of a personal level to help control the animal overpopulation problem.

1. You can adopt from your local animal shelter where spaying and neutering is required.

2. You can also support your local shelter by volunteering.

(TRANSITION: Any way that you can help reduce the number of unwanted animals by increasing awareness about spaying/neutering will do a bunch of animals a world of good.)

CONCLUSION

In conclusion, because the animal overpopulation problem has turned into a crisis, and the ways of controlling the problem aren't working anymore, it has become necessary to take personal responsibility for spaying/neutering to help control the problem more ethically, economically, and safely. It has also become necessary to call on the people of the community to put efforts forth to help with the problem any way that they can.
I would now like to read to you an excerpt from a pamphlet put out by The Fund for Animals.

"The time has come when it must no longer be acceptable to casually breed a dog or cat. Driving drunk kills, and is now a crime. Fur coats kill, and are falling from fashion. Smoking kills, and is becoming socially unacceptable. The Fund for Animals wants it to become taboo to not have a companion animal sterilized. Overpopulation kills, and accidental or purposeful breeding must fall from fashion and no longer be tolerated. It is a crime against the 10 to 12 million homeless dogs and cats we are killing every year."

Like the excerpt, the story of Apple does not have a happy ending either, at least not now, not at this moment. But, maybe this can change and Apple's fate could be different, because with the delivery of my speech today, I have hope that one person, or maybe two or three hears the cry for help -- and will act on it tomorrow.

BIBLIOGRAPHY

Fogle, B., D.V.M. Complete Dog Care Manual. New York: Dorling Kindersley Inc. 1993

Golden, L. "Animal Ownership Survey" distributed March 3, 1995, Speech 10, De Anza College.

Kilcommons, B. Good Owners, Great Dogs. New York: Warner Books Inc. 1992

Wolforth, M. G. Good Housekeeping Guide to Dog Care and Training. New York: Hearst Co. 1977.

_____. "Euthanasia is a Euphemism." Pamphlet. The Fund for Animals. April 1993.

"PREVENTION OF ATHEROSCLEROSIS"

By Vickee Cermak

INTRODUCTION

All of us in this room today have something in common. It is likely that we all have some degree of coronary artery disease, otherwise known as coronary atherosclerosis. Take a look at me. I'm thirty-one years old, and I was recently diagnosed as having artery disease. When my doctor told me that I had deposits in my arteries, I was scared and confused. I thought to myself, "Why me?" I have maintained a healthy lifestyle for the past thirteen years. I keep my weight down by following a low-fat diet and exercising regularly, and I don't smoke. I thought that atherosclerosis was a disease that affected the elderly. It wasn't until after I was diagnosed and researched the disease that I realized that it begins developing when we are very young. Among other things, the high fat diet my mother fed me, and the three packs a day of cigarette smoke my father exposed me to when I was growing up put me at risk. If my mother had been aware of the disease and its risk factors, she might have been able to prevent its development in me by changing my diet to a low-fat one, and if my father had known, maybe he wouldn't have smoked around me. I can't change the past and eliminate the disease, but because of my awareness of the disease and its risk factors, I can slow its progression. It's not too late for me, and it's not too late for any of you either.

PROPOSITION

In order to reduce the chances that we will have a heart attack or stroke, we must do three things. First, we must recognize that atherosclerosis begins developing when we are young; secondly, each of us must learn our personal risk factors for developing the disease; and finally, we must take action to reduce those risk factors.

BODY

I. In order to prevent heart attack and strokes, we must begin to view atherosclerosis as a disease of the young.

    A. According to Michael DeBakey M.D., a famous cardiologist, "Post-mortem studies carried out on young soldiers killed in the Korean War indicated that many of them had a significant degree of blockage due to atherosclerosis of the coronary arteries by the time they were in their mid-twenties."

    B. Autopsy studies were also conducted on 128 persons ranging in age from 3 to 26 who died in Bogalusa, Louisiana beginning in 1978.

        1. 56 of the 128 persons studied had evidence of coronary artery disease.

        2. This information is according to Gerald S. Berenson M.D. who is chief cardiologist of the Louisiana State University Medical Center and the director of the study.

    C. These studies indicate that it is likely that many of us in this room have some degree of coronary artery disease.

(TRANSITION: Do you know what your risk is of heart attack and stroke?)

II. In order to prevent heart attacks and strokes, we must determine our risk of developing atherosclerosis.

   A. According to the American Heart Association, the best way to determine your risk for developing atherosclerosis is to visit your physician and insist on risk factor screening for three major risk factors that don't cause any symptoms in the early stages.

      1. Have blood pressure checked at least every two years.

      2. Have a lipid profile done to check your blood cholesterol level at least every 5 years.

      3. Be screened for diabetes mellitus at least every 5 years.

   B. Many of us can't afford to see the doctor just for these tests, so here is a way to give you a start on learning your risk factors.

      1. Testing 1 2 3 in Valco Mall in Cupertino does free testing for cholesterol, blood pressure, and diabetes daily.

      2. After having your tests done, fill out the Risk Factor Pamphlet I gave you before the speech to give you a better idea of your risk for developing atherosclerosis.

(TRANSITION: So, what do we do after these tests?)

III. In order to prevent heart attacks and strokes, we must modify our lifestyle to reduce our risk of developing atherosclerosis.

   A. Obesity is a risk factor, so keep your weight down.

      1. One key is a low fat diet.

      2. Exercise vigorously at least 1/2 hour, three times a week.

   B. High blood pressure is a risk factor so have your blood pressure checked regularly either by your doctor or at your local drug store.

      1. If it is high, changing your diet, lowering your salt intake, and exercise can lower it.

      2. If that doesn't work, your doctor can prescribe medication to help keep your blood pressure within the normal range.

   C. Have your blood cholesterol checked every 5 years.

      1. If it is high, lowering your fat or cholesterol intake could lower it.

      2. If your high cholesterol level is a genetic factor, there are cholesterol-lowering drugs that your physician can prescribe to control it.

   D. If you smoke, stop, and if you don't smoke, don't start.

CONCLUSION

Atherosclerosis is seen as a disease affecting the old when in actuality it begins developing in early childhood, as early as infancy. In order to prevent the disease, we must change our thinking by viewing it as a disease of the young and begin preventative measures early in life. Now is the time. I've brought the disease to your attention and made you aware of the risk factors. Now, the rest is up to you. You can start preventative measures now and add years to your life, or you can continue what you are doing today, aid the progression of the disease and become a future heart attack or stroke statistic. There is another issue you should also consider -- your children's future. Start them out right from day one. Give them the chance at a long and healthy life. If you won't do it for yourself, do it for them. Prevent the development of this disease. It's all up to you.

BIBLIOGRAPHY

DeBakey, M., M.D. and Gotto, A., M.D. The Living Heart. New York: David McKay Co., Inc. 1977.

_____. "Cardiovascular Research Report." Pamphlet. American Heart Association. Summer 1989.

_____. "Coronary Risk Factor Statement for the American Public." Pamphlet. American Heart Association. 1987.

"STANDING FACE TO FACE WITH POVERTY"

By Sarah Jensen
(Reprinted with permission.)

INTRODUCTION

My heart was pounding as I knocked on the door to the one-roomed shack in the heart of Mexico's dump. I was excited that I had the opportunity to bring food to a poor family, but most of my anxiety stemmed from the fact that once the door opened, I knew I'd be standing face to face with poverty. As a tiny girl opened the door to her shack, my eyes awakened to the reality of poverty. She looked at me, startled to see a blond "gringa" at her door, but smiled as I handed her the food. As she yelled for her momma to come, I peeked into the small house, seeing temporary beds set up all over the dirt floor. The smells were unmistakable.

I had gotten a true glimpse of poverty. Poverty is not just a picture anymore. To me poverty is a real child living in cramped quarters smiling wide simply because of a small amount of generosity. Poverty to me is the mother of five young children who works from before the sun rises till after the sun sets in the fields with her husband and a baby strapped to her back.

Poverty to me has become a personal issue that touches me on a very personal level. I cannot think of world poverty without thinking of the faces and the souls it affects. I realize that most of you have not had the opportunity to visit poverty in action, but it is my sincere hope that after today, you can walk away with a better understanding of the very personal nature of poverty, and feel burdened, as I do, to take some course of action to put an end to it.

PROPOSITION

The issue of world hunger is an overwhelming one, however, there are courses of action to take that will help others live.

BODY

I. There are so many things that we can do to alleviate the issue of world hunger.

    A. Money is always the most useful, and least time consuming, way to help in the war against poverty, but as most of you indicated on my survey, you have a lot of excuses why this is not a viable option.

        1. The biggest reason for not donating to a charity is that you say you do not have enough money; however, seemingly insignificant amounts of money or time lead to significant changes in health and well being of many others.

        2. 15 cents a day would yield a $50 yearly gift which as you will find out later can drastically change the fate of an entire family in a third world country.

    B. If you still are convinced that you have absolutely no money to donate, please consider using your talents to help in the efforts.

        1. I have talked to many full time workers in different countries who are so appreciative for encouraging notes they receive from people back in the states.

     a.   These workers have an emotional full time job, and they, like us, are sometimes in need of a pick me up.

     b.   Your note could be just what they need to get through another day.

  2. There are also many other things that you can co.

     a.   Call or write the agency of your choice and ask what you specifically can do.

     b.   Give money, box food, write letters...the bottom line is to take action!

(Transition: Poverty will not go away if we choose to ignore it. For each moment that we postpone action, a person dies. Our resources do make a difference.)

II. To show you exactly how our resources make a difference, I want to trace our $50 donation through the channels of World Relief's Life Loan Program.

  A. World Relief is by far one of the best organizations I have come into contact with exemplifying good stewardship by using as much of their resources as possible.

    1. According to WR's 1990 annual report, of our hypothetical $50 donation, $8 would be used for overhead costs.

    2. The remaining $42 would be used by the people the money was originally intended for.

  B. That $42 could then be used for WR's Life Loan program which seeks to help women primarily start businesses so that they can create a steady income for their families.

    1. Under this program, women keep their pride and utilize their skills.

    2. The loans are issued through Community Banks sponsored by WR in varying denominations.

    3. On the woman's $42 loan (provided by us), she will be first given mandatory classes on how to start and manage a successful business.

    4. She will be charged an inflationary interest rate and the money is to be paid back in one year.

    5. The loan repayment rate in Monrovia, Liberia of 16 banks of 517 women stands at 100%.

    6. With these repaid loans, the banks are free to loan essentially the same money again and again.

    7. So, our $50 donation not only helps one woman and her family, but several women and several families!

  C. An article entitled "Liberia, A country Briefing" profiles many women who have benefited from this program.

    1. Annie Zwie, age 52 of Monrovia used her $42 loan to buy 100 lbs of flour and large quantities of sugar, baking powder and yeast.

a. Buying in bulk keeps her profit margin up and has allowed her to go from making 30 donuts a day to 105.

b. The money she has made has allowed her and her children to eat twice a day; her children have been able to attend school and she has money for hospital expenses.

2. Rebecca Johnson thinks she is about 20 and is a new mother in Logantown, Liberia.

a. She is waiting for funding so that she can start a business.

b. "If I had a loan," she says contemplating the future, "I'd go to the hospital when I am sick. I'd buy food. I'd keep a little for relatives who might stop by. Maybe I'd buy clothes for myself. Now I have nothing. I have no food. I'd like to buy meat, fish, pig's feet, but I can't buy that now," she says dismissing the thought.

CONCLUSION

Ever since I met that little girl several years ago I feel as though I met poverty. It touches me in a different way now--a personal one. To turn my back on the cries of poverty is in essence to turn my back on that little girl and all the others like her. Before we had little responsibility because of the fact that there was no ability to respond. But today, we know what is going on in other countries within a four second bounce off of a satellite. Therefore, it is our response--ability, our opportunity to save lives.

My challenge to you is to consider your "response--ability", your opportunity to save lives. Don't take it lightly. You can make a difference. As J. Brian Atwood says, "For every tragedy there are half a dozen islands of hope. Progress is still tentative, often fragile, which is precisely why we MUST NOT HESITATE NOW!"

BIBLIOGRAPHY

Cohen, M.J. (Ed.). 1995. Countries in Crisis. Maryland: Bread for the World Institute.

_____. "Liberia: A Country Briefing." Pamphlet. World Relief. Feb. 1996.

_____. "Mobilizing A Network of Hope." Pamphlet. World Relief. 1990.

_____. "World Relief Survival Catalog." Pamphlet. World Relief. 1995-96.

"PUTTING AN END TO DOMESTIC VIOLENCE"

By Emily Strong

INTRODUCTION

I have a friend who was a victim of domestic violence. At the beginning she was slapped by her batterer and abused verbally. She eventually got pregnant, hoping the baby would calm him down or make him love her, but it didn't. Over the following months the batterings escalated. "Sometimes he would whip her with an orange electrical cord, knotting it for greater impact. Her body would spasm from the lashings and she'd frantically try to catch the cord with her bare hands before it could strike again." At night he would lock her in her room so that she couldn't get away, call her mom, or call the police. Finally, when her baby was a few months old, my friend ran for her life. She threw a few things in a blanket for the baby, climbed out the bathroom window and ran, never to return to the abuse again. With the help of her family and friends, she put her abuser behind bars. On January 14, 1996, her story was put into print in the San Francisco Examiner Magazine. (Fernandez, Elizabeth. "Lila's Story, a True Tale of Crime, Punishment and Courage." San Francisco Examiner Magazine. January 14, 1996.) In the survey that I took on March 6, 1996, fourteen of you said that you knew someone, either directly or indirectly, who is in a violent relationship. According to a statistic in the National Women's Health Report September/October 1992, violence will occur at least once in two thirds of all marriages, and that is not including non-married couples. So, chances are you might come across a violent relationship in your life, and it is important to know what you should do in these situations.

PROPOSITION

Domestic violence is a giant problem in our society and can't be stopped until we are all educated on the myths about domestic violence, know where to call to assist both the batterer and the victim to seek help, and know what you can do to help someone get out of a violent relationship.

(TRANSITION: So, lets begin by getting rid of some of the stereotypes you might have about domestic violence.)

BODY

I. In order to stop the cycle of domestic violence, we must first know all the truths about some common myths about domestic violence and why they are indeed myths. (Taken from: Domestic Abuse, Violence Between Couples)

    A. Myth #1: "If he really wanted to stop, he would."

        1. Truth: Many abusers hate themselves for what they do and honestly grieve over their behavior--and are still unable to prevent themselves from doing it again.

        2. Truth: Therapy is the only way to gain the self-respect that is the basis for giving others the respect that makes abuse impossible.

    B. Myth #2: "The sons of wife beaters see how awful things are and grow up to treat women differently."

1. Truth: Family history is often repeated and not changed, so unless professional help is given, the cycle continues.

2. Truth: The child sees that those who are hurt keep getting hurt, and sees the person who does the hurting less vulnerable, the child has learned no other means of expressing himself and so uses violence as a means of expression.

C. Myth #3: "Spouse abuse is a problem and a product of the lower class, especially those in poverty."

   1. Truth: Some researchers believe that not as much abuse is found in the middle and upper classes, because people don't want to find it.

   2. Truth: Women in the upper class have images to uphold; lower class women feel as if they don't have as much to lose.

   3. Truth: Upper class women risk giving up economic security and social standing; they have a lot to lose by reporting.

D. Myth #4: "Only the mentally ill do it."

   1. Truth: Less than one in 10 abusers have a mental illness.

   2. Truth: Violence occurs because the individual doesn't see alternatives and doesn't know what else to do.

E. Myth #5: "What goes on in someone else's home is `None of my business.'"

   1. Truth: Many people think, "If they want to live that way, let them." Violence is not a rational choice; its presence is an indication of a family out of control.

   2. Truth: We have a responsibility to help when people are endangering others, particularly when victims cannot protect themselves.

(TRANSITION: Now that you know that domestic violence occurs throughout society, I want to urge you to call someone if you know of a violent relationship.)

II. Since my survey showed that about half of you know where to call for the victim or for the batterer and the other half did not know where to call at all, it is important to me that ALL of you know where to call.

A. There are hotlines you could call to help both the victim and the batterer.

   1. The National Domestic Violence Hotline: (800) 333-7233 is there to give information and help.

   2. Support Network for Battered Women: (415) 940-7855 is there for support information and resources.

   3. Male batterers' program: (415) 962-7855 is there to help batterers learn to deal with their emotions in a non-violent way.

203

B. There are also 1,400 battered women's hotlines, shelters, and safe-homes nationwide that provide: 1) Crisis intervention, 2) Legal, economic housing and medical care, and, 3) Community education and professional training.

(TRANSITION: Now that you know where to go, or who to call to help someone in a violent relationship, you need to know what to do or say.)

III. There are many things you can do if you are in a violent relationship or as a friend of a victim or of a batterer.

    A. If the person you love is using threats, coercion or physical violence to frighten you and control your actions you need to do several things.

        1. Make a safety plan in case you need to leave quickly.

        2. Tell someone you trust.

        3. Know that you are not alone and that support is available.

        4. Remember that no one deserves abuse; you are not responsible for your partner's violence and abuse.

    B. If you know a woman who is being abused you need to do several things.

        1. Believe her.

        2. Understand that leaving an abusive relationship is difficult.

        3. Tell her that the violence is not her fault.

        4. Encourage her to get help. (Pamphlet: Support Network for Women)

    C. If you know a batterer you can do two things.

        1. Call the male batterer hotline.

        2. Encourage him to seek help.

CONCLUSION

With this information that I have given you today regarding the false myths about domestic violence, who you can call to get help, and the things you can do or say to help, you will be able to make essential decisions if you are ever faced with a violent relationship, whether it is you or someone you care about. The only real way to end a violent relationship is to get out of the relationship and seek help, because violent relationships will never heal themselves.

BIBLIOGRAPHY

Fernandez, E. "Lila's Story, a True Tale of Crime, Punishment and Courage." <u>San Francisco Examiner Magazine</u>. January 14, 1996.

_____. "Domestic Abuse: Violence Between Couples." Life Skills Education, Inc. 1992.

_____. "Domestic Violence." National Women's Health Report. September/October 1992.

_____. "No One Deserves Abuse!" Pamphlet. Support Network for Battered Women. Mountain View, CA. 1996.

ASSIGNMENT: Peer Editing of Speech Outline

SPEAKER_____ PEER EDITOR_____

INSTRUCTIONS: As the speaker delivers the speech from manuscript, check the following:

1) From the list on page 149 circle the type(s) of Attention Device(s) you heard in the introduction. Rhetorical Questions, Illustration/Anecdotes, Startling Statement, Quotation, Humor, Action, None, Other (explain):

2) What did the speaker say in the credibility statement?

3) Write out the proposition

4) Count and list the sources cited during the speech.

   NONE
   1.
   2.
   3.
   4.

5) Using page 134, identify 3 to 5 types of supporting information used in the speech and write a few words to indicate how they are used.
   1.

   2.

   3.

   4.

   5.

6) Give examples where the speaker uses the persuasive proofs in the speech.
   Logos:

   Pathos:

   Ethos:

7) How does the speaker use the Audience Analysis in the Speech? Give examples

8) From the list on page 149 circle the type(s) of Clincher(s) you heard in the conclusion. Rhetorical Questions, Illustration/Anecdotes, Startling Statement, Quotation, Humor, Action, None, Other (explain):

Cover Sheet: **Persuasive Speech Outline**

PERSUASIVE SPEECH EVALUATION (INSTRUCTOR EVALUATION)

STUDENT SPEAKER_____

THE SPEECH ITSELF
    INTRODUCTION   (12)_____
        Attention Device
        Credibility Statement

    THESIS (PROPOSITION)   (5)_____
        Introduce Topic

    BODY
        CLEAR ARGUMENTS   (10)_____
            Easy to Hear
            Clear Transition
            Organization Clear
        SUPPORTING INFORMATION   (20)_____
            Concrete Examples
            Concrete Evidence
            Appropriate Sources (cited in speech)
            Use of Language
        ATTEMPT AT PERSUASION   (30)_____
            Clearly Defined
            Clear Direction
            Appropriate use of Logos, Pathos, Ethos
            Use of Audience Analysis

    CONCLUSION   (12)_____
        Summary
        Clincher

    DELIVERY   (20)_____
        Extemporaneous
        Natural
        Good use of Eye Contact
        No Distracting Movement or Sounds
        Appropriate Voice Volume
        Appropriate Voice Pitch (Not a monotone)
        Appropriate Speaking Rate

    OVERALL EFFECT   (11)_____

                                   TOTAL: (120)_____
STRENGTHS

SUGGESTIONS

Critique Form: **Persuasive Speech**

SPEAKER:_____

TOPIC:_____

	POOR	FAIR	BELOW AVERAGE	AVERAGE	ABOVE AVERAGE	EXCELLENT	SUPERIOR	COMMENTS
CHOICE OF SUBJECT: Appropriate to speaker, listener, assignment, time limit	1	2	3	4	5	6	7	
ORGANIZATION: Clear, simple, orderly, logical, easy to follow	1	2	3	4	5	6	7	
DEVELOPMENT OF INTRODUCTION: Did it gain an attentive, appropriate, intelligent hearing?	1	2	3	4	5	6	7	
DEVELOPMENT OF DISCUSSION: Factual, visual support, appropriate support	1	2	3	4	5	6	7	
ATTEMPT AT PERSUASION: Logical, clear, evidence of some technique or "goal" to speech	1	2	3	4	5	6	7	
DEVELOPMENT OF CONCLUSION: Summary, appeal	1	2	3	4	5	6	7	
BODILY CONTROL: Facial expression, eye contact, gestures, posture, any movement	1	2	3	4	5	6	7	
CONSIDERING THE AUDIENCE: Rapport, communicativeness	1	2	3	4	5	6	7	
LANGUAGE: Clarity, vividness, impressiveness	1	2	3	4	5	6	7	
VOICE AND PRONUNCIATION: Appropriate	1	2	3	4	5	6	7	
ATTITUDES: Toward listeners and speaking situation, urge to communicate, urge to persuade	1	2	3	4	5	6	7	
OVERALL EFFECTIVENESS Write a one or two sentence evaluation.	1	2	3	4	5	6	7	

CRITIC_____

(YOUR NAME WILL BE REMOVED)

Critique Form: Persuasive Speech

SPEAKER:_____

TOPIC:_____

	POOR	FAIR	BELOW AVERAGE	AVERAGE	ABOVE AVERAGE	EXCELLENT	SUPERIOR	COMMENTS

CHOICE OF SUBJECT: Appropriate to speaker, listener, assignment, time limit   1 2 3 4 5 6 7

ORGANIZATION: Clear, simple, orderly, logical, easy to follow   1 2 3 4 5 6 7

DEVELOPMENT OF INTRODUCTION: Did it gain an attentive, appropriate, intelligent hearing?   1 2 3 4 5 6 7

DEVELOPMENT OF DISCUSSION: Factual, visual support, appropriate support   1 2 3 4 5 6 7

ATTEMPT AT PERSUASION: Logical, clear, evidence of some technique or "goal" to speech   1 2 3 4 5 6 7

DEVELOPMENT OF CONCLUSION: Summary, appeal   1 2 3 4 5 6 7

BODILY CONTROL: Facial expression, eye contact, gestures, posture, any movement   1 2 3 4 5 6 7

CONSIDERING THE AUDIENCE: Rapport, communicativeness   1 2 3 4 5 6 7

LANGUAGE: Clarity, vividness, impressiveness   1 2 3 4 5 6 7

VOICE AND PRONUNCIATION: Appropriate   1 2 3 4 5 6 7

ATTITUDES: Toward listeners and speaking situation, urge to communicate, urge to persuade   1 2 3 4 5 6 7

OVERALL EFFECTIVENESS
Write a one or two sentence evaluation.   1 2 3 4 5 6 7

CRITIC_____
(YOUR NAME WILL BE REMOVED)

Critique Form: **Persuasive Speech**

SPEAKER:_____

TOPIC:_____

	POOR	FAIR	BELOW AVERAGE	AVERAGE	ABOVE AVERAGE	EXCELLENT	SUPERIOR	COMMENTS
CHOICE OF SUBJECT: Appropriate to speaker, listener, assignment, time limit	1	2	3	4	5	6	7	
ORGANIZATION: Clear, simple, orderly, logical, easy to follow	1	2	3	4	5	6	7	
DEVELOPMENT OF INTRODUCTION: Did it gain an attentive, appropriate, intelligent hearing?	1	2	3	4	5	6	7	
DEVELOPMENT OF DISCUSSION: Factual, visual support, appropriate support	1	2	3	4	5	6	7	
ATTEMPT AT PERSUASION: Logical, clear, evidence of some technique or "goal" to speech	1	2	3	4	5	6	7	
DEVELOPMENT OF CONCLUSION: Summary, appeal	1	2	3	4	5	6	7	
BODILY CONTROL: Facial expression, eye contact, gestures, posture, any movement	1	2	3	4	5	6	7	
CONSIDERING THE AUDIENCE: Rapport, communicativeness	1	2	3	4	5	6	7	
LANGUAGE: Clarity, vividness, impressiveness	1	2	3	4	5	6	7	
VOICE AND PRONUNCIATION: Appropriate	1	2	3	4	5	6	7	
ATTITUDES: Toward listeners and speaking situation, urge to communicate, urge to persuade	1	2	3	4	5	6	7	
OVERALL EFFECTIVENESS Write a one or two sentence evaluation.	1	2	3	4	5	6	7	

CRITIC_____

(YOUR NAME WILL BE REMOVED)

Critique Form: **Persuasive Speech**

SPEAKER:_____

TOPIC:_____

	POOR	FAIR	BELOW AVERAGE	AVERAGE	ABOVE AVERAGE	EXCELLENT	SUPERIOR	COMMENTS
CHOICE OF SUBJECT: Appropriate to speaker, listener, assignment, time limit	1	2	3	4	5	6	7	
ORGANIZATION: Clear, simple, orderly, logical, easy to follow	1	2	3	4	5	6	7	
DEVELOPMENT OF INTRODUCTION: Did it gain an attentive, appropriate, intelligent hearing?	1	2	3	4	5	6	7	
DEVELOPMENT OF DISCUSSION: Factual, visual support, appropriate support	1	2	3	4	5	6	7	
ATTEMPT AT PERSUASION: Logical, clear, evidence of some technique or "goal" to speech	1	2	3	4	5	6	7	
DEVELOPMENT OF CONCLUSION: Summary, appeal	1	2	3	4	5	6	7	
BODILY CONTROL: Facial expression, eye contact, gestures, posture, any movement	1	2	3	4	5	6	7	
CONSIDERING THE AUDIENCE: Rapport, communicativeness	1	2	3	4	5	6	7	
LANGUAGE: Clarity, vividness, impressiveness	1	2	3	4	5	6	7	
VOICE AND PRONUNCIATION: Appropriate	1	2	3	4	5	6	7	
ATTITUDES: Toward listeners and speaking situation, urge to communicate, urge to persuade	1	2	3	4	5	6	7	
OVERALL EFFECTIVENESS Write a one or two sentence evaluation.	1	2	3	4	5	6	7	

CRITIC_____

(YOUR NAME WILL BE REMOVED)

Critique Form: **Persuasive Speech**

SPEAKER:_____

TOPIC:_____

	POOR	FAIR	BELOW AVERAGE	AVERAGE	ABOVE AVERAGE	EXCELLENT	SUPERIOR	COMMENTS
CHOICE OF SUBJECT: Appropriate to speaker, listener, assignment, time limit	1	2	3	4	5	6	7	
ORGANIZATION: Clear, simple, orderly, logical, easy to follow	1	2	3	4	5	6	7	
DEVELOPMENT OF INTRODUCTION: Did it gain an attentive, appropriate, intelligent hearing?	1	2	3	4	5	6	7	
DEVELOPMENT OF DISCUSSION: Factual, visual support, appropriate support	1	2	3	4	5	6	7	
ATTEMPT AT PERSUASION: Logical, clear, evidence of some technique or "goal" to speech	1	2	3	4	5	6	7	
DEVELOPMENT OF CONCLUSION: Summary, appeal	1	2	3	4	5	6	7	
BODILY CONTROL: Facial expression, eye contact, gestures, posture, any movement	1	2	3	4	5	6	7	
CONSIDERING THE AUDIENCE: Rapport, communicativeness	1	2	3	4	5	6	7	
LANGUAGE: Clarity, vividness, impressiveness	1	2	3	4	5	6	7	
VOICE AND PRONUNCIATION: Appropriate	1	2	3	4	5	6	7	
ATTITUDES: Toward listeners and speaking situation, urge to communicate, urge to persuade	1	2	3	4	5	6	7	
OVERALL EFFECTIVENESS Write a one or two sentence evaluation.	1	2	3	4	5	6	7	

CRITIC_____

(YOUR NAME WILL BE REMOVED)

Critique Form: **Persuasive Speech**

SPEAKER:_____

TOPIC:_____

	POOR	FAIR	BELOW AVERAGE	AVERAGE	ABOVE AVERAGE	EXCELLENT	SUPERIOR	COMMENTS
CHOICE OF SUBJECT: Appropriate to speaker, listener, assignment, time limit	1	2	3	4	5	6	7	
ORGANIZATION: Clear, simple, orderly, logical, easy to follow	1	2	3	4	5	6	7	
DEVELOPMENT OF INTRODUCTION: Did it gain an attentive, appropriate, intelligent hearing?	1	2	3	4	5	6	7	
DEVELOPMENT OF DISCUSSION: Factual, visual support, appropriate support	1	2	3	4	5	6	7	
ATTEMPT AT PERSUASION: Logical, clear, evidence of some technique or "goal" to speech	1	2	3	4	5	6	7	
DEVELOPMENT OF CONCLUSION: Summary, appeal	1	2	3	4	5	6	7	
BODILY CONTROL: Facial expression, eye contact, gestures, posture, any movement	1	2	3	4	5	6	7	
CONSIDERING THE AUDIENCE: Rapport, communicativeness	1	2	3	4	5	6	7	
LANGUAGE: Clarity, vividness, impressiveness	1	2	3	4	5	6	7	
VOICE AND PRONUNCIATION: Appropriate	1	2	3	4	5	6	7	
ATTITUDES: Toward listeners and speaking situation, urge to communicate, urge to persuade	1	2	3	4	5	6	7	
OVERALL EFFECTIVENESS Write a one or two sentence evaluation.	1	2	3	4	5	6	7	

CRITIC_____

(YOUR NAME WILL BE REMOVED)

ASSIGNMENT: Personal Evaluation Form for Persuasive Speech

COMPLETE THIS FORM AFTER YOU VIEW THE VIDEO TAPE OF YOUR SPEECH

NAME_____

SPEECH TITLE_____

1. Why did you choose this persuasive speech topic?

2. What was your specific goal?

3. Attach a copy of your Audience Analysis and the tally of the results. What did you learn from the analysis that helped you in preparing the speech?

4. List specific ways in which you adapted this speech to this audience.

5. How well did you achieve your purpose and goal? (Both from your response to viewing the tape and from audience reactions)

6. What points of evidence did you use to prove your proposition? How effective were your points of evidence?

7. Were you persuasive? Did you meet your own expectations about your persuasive abilities?

8. What points about your delivery impress you as you view your speech on tape?

9. If you could deliver the speech again, what one point would you change?

ASSIGNMENT: The Public Service Announcement (PSA)

Contributed by Rob Dewis, De Anza College. (Reprinted with permission.)

You have decided to take advantage of a television station's invitation to speak out on an issue that concerns you. You will write and deliver 5 to 6 sentences, using the Motivated Sequence Design (add a Clincher, if you wish) that will express the problem and your suggestion for <u>action</u>. Keep in mind that you will be talking to an audience "through" the lens of a camera.

Suggestions:
- choose a problem that interests you
- think in terms of the Motivated Sequence Design method
- write only one sentence for each of the following steps (5 to 6 sentences)

MOTIVATED SEQUENCE DESIGN
     ATTENTION STEP
     NEED STEP (What is the problem?)
     SATISFACTION STEP (What is the solution?)
     VISUALIZATION STEP
     ACTION STEP (Be specific.)
     CLINCHER (Optional.)

REQUIREMENTS:
     SCRIPT: The steps listed above, each followed by your sentence for that step
     VISUAL AID: At least one, used effectively
     TIME: 15 to 60 seconds (Practice and time yourself.)

- - - - - - - - - - -
INSTRUCTORS:
     Show examples of well-done and not-so-well done PSAs that you have recorded from television. I also record myself doing three or four versions of a PSA, starting poorly, and improving with each one.

GOALS
1. Applying the creative use of concise language.
2. Becoming familiar with, and applying, the Motivated Sequence Design.
3. Developing a sensitivity to an unseen and diverse audience; the television viewers.
4. Applying the skills learned in public speaking to the mediated communication context.
5. Focusing, through an extremely concentrated experience, on a primary goal of speaking in a public context; effectively communicating a planned and prepared message.

The students should write, re-write, practice, and re-write the PSA a number of times, paying special attention to the way "oral" language is different from "written" language.

The students, when looking into the camera, should picture the individual persons they are trying to reach, and concentrate on the import of their message rather than being unduly concerned with the camera.

When recording the students' PSAs, I give them two or three tries.

After recording the entire class, watch the PSAs, scanning through false starts, and pausing at the end of each PSA to elicit student comments.

Demo Script: PSA Assignment

Motivated Sequence Design
Note: Television scripts are written in upper case.

ATTENTION STEP: AN OLD SAYING GOES, "IF YOU CAN'T SAY SOMETHING NICE, DON'T SAY ANYTHING AT ALL"

NEED STEP: THE PROBLEM WITH THAT PHILOSOPHY IS THAT WITH ALL THE BIG AND LITTLE PROBLEMS WE ENCOUNTER IN LIFE, YOU MIGHT SPEND MOST OF YOUR TIME NOT SAYING ANYTHING AT ALL.

SATISFACTION STEP: HERE AT DE ANZA COLLEGE WE HAVE SOME SPEECH CLASSES THAT'LL HELP YOU LEARN TO SAY WHAT YOU WANT AND NEED TO SAY TO BE MORE SUCCESSFUL IN YOUR SCHOOL, SOCIAL, BUSINESS, AND FAMILY LIFE.

VISUALIZATION STEP: YOU CAN LEARN TO COMMUNICATE MORE EFFECTIVELY AND MORE CONFIDENTLY WHETHER YOU'RE SPEAKING TO ONE, OR ONE THOUSAND.

ACTION STEP: YOU CAN FIND THESE COURSES (hold up page from Class Schedule) LISTED UNDER SPEECH IN THE DE ANZA COLLEGE SCHEDULE SO YOU CAN REGISTER FOR THE COURSE AND TIME THAT WORKS FOR YOU.

CLINCHER: (OPTIONAL) YOU MIGHT SAY THE NEW OLD SAYING IS, "IF YOU CAN'T SAY SOMETHING NICE, AT LEAST LEARN TO SAY IT WELL."

Cover Sheet: Public Service Announcement

PSA EVALUATION (INSTRUCTOR EVALUATION)

STUDENT SPEAKER_____

REQUIREMENTS (Criteria for Evaluation):

CONTENT
- timely and timeless
- interesting and well thought out
- demonstrates Ethos, Logos, and Pathos
- appropriate for context
- only one sentence allowed for each step in the Motivated Sequence Design

ORGANIZATION
- typed, full-sentence script
    Attention Step
    Need Step
    Satisfaction Step
    Visualization Step
    Action Step
    Clincher (optional)

DELIVERY
- extemporaneous (may memorize, but delivery should not seem "automated")
- contact "through" the camera lens
- established credibility
- clear distinction between steps of Motivated Sequence Design
- vocal and physical variety

VISUAL AID
- at least one, used effectively

TIME
- between 15 and 60 seconds

GRADES: PRESENTATION:_____(40)

            OUTLINE:_____(20)

ASSIGNMENT: Speech Critique

For this project you are asked to find a speech that interest you and critique it. You are required to work with the **written text** of the speech in order to fully analyze it. Your paper should be organized around three parts. Below is an explanation of what you may want to include in each of the three parts. The paper should be 4 pages typed, double-spaced.

INTRODUCTION
Orient the reader to the speaker's background, experience, ethos. Orient the reader to the speech (when, where, why and how did it take place, what is its social context or historical significance). Who is the audience? What is the purpose of the speech?

THESIS STATEMENT
Preview the main points you will cover. For example, "In this paper I will critique Martin Luther King's 'I have a dream' speech based on language and style, delivery, and use of identification."

BODY
Begin by defining the terms you have chosen as points of critique. Explain the term before you begin to apply it in your analysis. Thoroughly develop the main points you have previewed. Support your assertions with quotations from the speech text you have chosen. Give as many examples as you can. Adhere to college level of style, form, presentation, and citation. It is appropriate to include what others think about the speech if you choose. In that case, remember to cite your sources and include a list of references. Avoid simply summarizing the speech. Assume the reader has read the speech; your paper is a critical analysis.

Ideas for main points include any topic we have studied this term: Ethos, Pathos, Logos, Identification, Organization, Language and Style, Delivery, Vocal Delivery (if you are able to see video, and/or hear audio), Supporting Information, Audience Analysis, etc.

CONCLUSION
Simply restate your main ideas in different words. Highlight your favorite parts of your paper. Make some concluding remarks about the effectiveness or ineffectiveness of the speech based on your critique. Did the speaker achieve his or her purpose? In this section, it is appropriate if you wish, to include any personal feelings or ideas about the speech.

GUIDELINES
This paper is to be typed in essay format using transitions, **not labels** (as in an outline). Do not skip spaces between paragraphs as a substitute for connectives. Your paper should have a title and heading. Staple in the upper left and avoid folders, bindings. Proofread your paper.

SUGGESTIONS FOR FINDING A SPEECH
Start with a speaker, subject, culture, period in history, or social movement that interest you. Begin searching for a speech with your area of interest in mind. Best suggestion for finding a speech text: Vital Speeches of the Day available in the campus library. Internet searches also yield useful information. Key words: Great Speeches, Presidential rhetoric, Commencement speeches.

Copy of Written Speech Due to Instructor_____

Critical Analysis Paper Due _____

Example: **Speech delivered by Dr. Martin Luther King Jr. in 1963**

I HAVE A DREAM

Five score years ago, a great American, in whose symbolic shadow we stand today, signed the Emancipation Proclamation. This momentous decree came as a great beacon of light and hope to millions of Negro slaves who had been seared in the flames of withering injustice. It came as the joyous daybreak to end the long night of captivity.

But one hundred years later, the Negro still is not free. One hundred years later, the life of the Negro is still sadly crippled by the manacle of segregation and the chain of discrimination. One hundred years later, the Negro lives on a lonely island of poverty in the midst of a vast ocean of material prosperity. One hundred years later, the Negro is till languishing in the corner of American society and finds himself an exile in his own land. So we have come here today to dramatize a shameful condition.

In a sense we have come to the Capital to cash a check. When the architects of our republic wrote the magnificent words of the Constitution and the Declaration of Independence, they were signing a promissory note to which every American was to fall heir. This note was a promise that all men -- black men as well as white men -- would be guaranteed the unalienable right of life, liberty, and the pursuit of happiness.

But it is obvious today that America has defaulted on this promissory note insofar as her citizens of color are concerned. Instead of honoring this sacred obligation, America has given the Negro people a bad check -- a check that has come back marked "insufficient funds." But we refuse to believe that the bank of justice is bankrupt. We refuse to believe that there are insufficient funds in the great vaults of opportunity in the Nation.

So we have come to cash this check -- a check that will give us the riches of freedom and the security of justice.

We have also come to this hallowed spot to remind America that the fierce urgency is now. There is not time to engage in the luxury of cooling off or to take the tranquilizing drug of gradualism. Now is the time to make real the promise of democracy. Now is the time to rise from the dark and desolate valley of segregation to the sunlit path of racial justice. Now is the time to lift our Nation from the quicksand of racial injustice to the solid rock of brotherhood. Now is the time to make justice a reality for all of God's children.

I say to you today, my friends, even though we face the difficulties of today and tomorrow, I still have a dream. It is a dream deeply rooted in the American dream. I have a dream that one day this Nation will rise up and live out the true meaning of its creed -- "we hold these truths to be self-evident that all men are created equal."

I have a dream that one day on the red hills of Georgia the sons of slaves and the sons of former slave owners will be able to sit down together at the table of brotherhood. I have a dream that one day even the state of Mississippi, sweltering with the heat of injustice, sweltering with the heat of oppression, will be transformed into an oasis of freedom and justice.

I have a dream that my four little children will one day live in a Nation where they will not be judged by the color of their skins, but by the conduct of their character.

I have a dream that one day in Alabama, with this vicious racist, its Governor, having his lips dripping the words of interposition and nullification -- one day right there in Alabama, little black boys and black girls will be able to join hands with little white boys and girls as brothers and sisters.

I have a dream that one day every valley shall be exalted; every hill and mountain shall be made low, the rough places will be made plane, the crooked places will be made straight, and the glory of the Lord shall be revealed, and all flesh shall see it together.

This will be the day -- this will be the day when all of God's children will be able to sing with new meaning, "My country 'tis of thee, sweet land of liberty, of thee I sing. Land where my fathers died, land of the pilgrim's pride, from every mountainside, let freedom ring..."

So let freedom ring from the prodigious hilltops of New Hampshire. Let freedom ring from the mighty mountains of New York. Let freedom ring from the heightening Alleghenies of Pennsylvania!

Let freedom ring from the snowcapped Rockies of Colorado! Let freedom ring from the curvaceous slopes of California!

But not only that. Let freedom ring from Stone Mountain of Georgia!

Let freedom ring from Lookout Mountain of Tennessee!

Let freedom ring from every hill and molehill of Mississippi. From every mountainside, let freedom ring.

And when this happens, when we allow freedom to ring -- when we let it ring from every village and every hamlet, from every state and every city -- we will be able to speed up that day when all of God's children, black men and white men, Jews and Gentiles, Protestants and Catholics, will be able to join hands and sing in the words of the old Negro spiritual, "Free at last! Free at last! Thank God Almighty, we are free at last!"

BIBLIOGRAPHY

Brower, K. "Profile of the Serial Killer." Informative Speech for Speech 10, Collaborative Learning Class, De Anza College, Summer 1998.

Cermak, V. J. "Prevention of Atherosclerosis." Persuasive Speech for Speech 10, Collaborative Learning Class, De Anza College, Fall 1990.

Dewis, R. De Anza College, Cupertino, CA. "PSA Assignment."

Endter, S. De Anza College, Cupertino, CA. "Ideas for Using Visual/Audio Aids."

Golden, L. "Taking Care of Man's Best Friend" and "The Cry for Help." Informative and Persuasive Speeches for Speech 10, Collaborative Learning Class, De Anza College, Winter 1995.

Jensen, S. "Standing Face to Face With Poverty." Persuasive Speech for Speech 10, Collaborative Learning Class, De Anza College, Winter 1996.

Mickwee, J. "Audience Analysis Survey." Example for Speech 10, Collaborative Learning Class, De Anza College, Summer 1998.

Miller, G. C. West Valley College, Saratoga, CA. "Outlining Instructions." Adapted from materials prepared as Handouts in various speech courses.

Mudd, C. S. and Sillars M. O. 1991. Public Speaking: Content and Communication. Sixth Edition. Prospect Heights, IL: Waveland Press.

Ryan, H.R. 1987. American Rhetoric from Roosevelt to Reagan. Prospect Heights: Waveland Press.

Sprague, J. and Stuart, D. 2000. The Speaker's Handbook. Fifth Edition. Fort Worth, TX. Harcourt Brace Jovanovich, Pub.

Strong, E. "Putting an End to Domestic Violence." Persuasive Speech for Speech 10, Collaborative Learning Class, De Anza College, Winter 1996.

Tedford, K. De Anza College, Cupertino, CA. "Using Research as Supporting Information." Rewrite.

Typaldos, C. "Statue of Liberty." Informative Speech for Speech 10, Collaborative Learning Class, De Anza College, Summer 1998.

Williams, M. Williams Baptist College, Walnut Ridge, AR. "Attention Device and Clincher" and "Delivery." Written by invitation for inclusion in this workbook.